Angela Reinhardt

POINTE SHOES
TIPS & TRICKS

for choosing, tuning and care

dance books

Original title: "Der passende Spitzenschuh"
published by Henschel Verlag, Berlin / Germany

English edition first published in 2008 by Dance Books Ltd,
The Old Bakery, 4 Lenten Street, Alton, Hampshire GU34 1HG

ISBN: 978-1852-731151

English translation: Jeremy Leslie-Spinks

Editorial assistance: Karin Schmidt-Feister, Mike-Martin Robacki
Picture credits: All paintings and drawings by Christina Norström Blankstein.
Photos: Mike-Martin Robacki
Photos on pp. 07, 10 by Arwid Lagenpusch, portrait on p. 109 by Ada Kim,
rear cover portrait by Frank Zauritz
Layout & composition: Mike-Martin Robacki

Printed by Latimer Trend Ltd., Plymouth, UK

CONTENTS

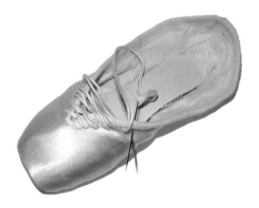

INTRODUCTION

Ever since I was a ballet student, I have always been fascinated by the idea of being able to dance on pointe, in hovering perfection. In order to be able to dance "perfectly" I spent a lot of time looking for the "perfect" shoe. I was constantly experimenting with different ways of tying, sewing and changing my shoes. I tried out different makes and styles of shoes. I wanted them to be less painful, wanted my feet to look more beautiful, to show off my instep to better advantage, to improve stability, to reduce the noise of the blocks – an endless list of wishes. I asked my teachers, I got together with other students to operate on my shoes. We literally dismembered the shoes until all the component parts lay before us in our attempts to find out at last the secret of the "perfect" pointe shoe.

During my dancing career I adopted the tricks and methods of other ballerinas, and tried out many modifications together with the shoe-makers. I was still hoping that one day I might perhaps find the "perfect" shoe for me. I was never entirely satisfied; there was always something to cut, to sew or to improve.

At last it gradually dawned on me. There's no such thing as "the perfect pointe-shoe"! If there were, it would have to mean that all the circumstances surrounding dancers and dancing were always the same.

People's feet would always have to be the same size, with the same level of circulation, and always the same thickness, no matter whether the foot in question were fresh and rested, or had just got through two hours of *Swan Lake*. Even the various floor-coverings are often completely different from each other in terms of the friction or smoothness of the surface.

Almost always, stages and ballet studio floors differ in their construction; sometimes they cushion your landings, other times they're as hard as concrete. On tour, dancers have to contend with all sorts of different conditions in the various theatres, and pointe shoes must be readjusted to cope with each new situation.

There is no such thing as the "perfect" shoe. However, years of searching for it have taught me many tricks and ways of adapting the shoe. Armed with this knowledge, I was finally able to create an "almost-perfect" shoe to meet the demands of many differing situations. Sometimes, though, their "near-perfection" didn't last past the interval. The idea of a "perfect" pair of pointe shoes always comes down to interaction between the prevailing conditions and our ability to react appropriately to change.

"Every journey, however short or long, starts with the first step."

Asian proverb

This book is meant to provide you with the craftsmanship which can help you adjust your shoes in the best possible ways to cope with varying conditions. I would also like to share with you some of my experience of precautions to safeguard your health, and offer some guidance for helping yourself. You're almost certain to find a couple of helpful suggestions.

I had the idea for this book while I was engaged as Principal Dancer at the Komische Oper in Berlin. In order to dance all my numerous performances and principal rôles as well as I could, I had to dedicate many hours of fine-tuning to my pointe shoes, the tools of my trade.

Oh, how often I have cursed, thrown the shoes against the wall, stabbed myself in the finger or cut myself. Tears and drops of blood flowed liberally. Even so, there is something very calming in all this work on the shoes, the pottering, the not-yet-quite-rightness, the trying and the tying. It was a wonderful help to me, for example, when I was trying to come to grips with stage-fright. Also, working on a pair of pointe shoes is somehow a way of getting to know each other. Because of all the attention I pay them, they become almost a part of me, like a second skin. Onstage, I have to be able to rely on them completely.

Even today, I'm still constantly finding and trying out new tricks and ways to facilitate dancing in pointe shoes for myself. I've looked through so many books and so much teaching material in search of information on the properties of the pointe shoe or the possible way to modify and adapt it. I was disappointed, however, to find that so far, not nearly enough attention seems to have been paid to this essential tool of our trade. Again and again, I meet dancers, students, teachers and parents who are beset by unsolved problems or unanswered questions about pointe shoes.

After much encouragement and a great many requests to put my more than 25 years of pointe shoe experience at the disposal of all the "needy" in written form, I finally decided the time had come to tackle this guidebook.

Of course to start with, it won't be easy among so many modifications and techniques, for you to find the right choice that will work for your shoes and your feet. Perhaps the one you choose will be spot on, then again perhaps not. Simply try out the possibilities this book suggests. Your feet will be grateful, and you'll definitely feel better on pointe from now on.

Yours,

"Am I talented enough?"

I'm sure you're going to ask yourself this question. Maybe you don't really believe you have enough talent to dance, nor even to study to be a professional. Maybe you think you don't have the "ideal" body, or you're hesitating because you haven't been in a children's dance group, or learned gymnastics, or done figure-skating. Then let me tell you something.

Most important of all is your interest, your sense of commitment, and your passion for dancing. With these, you can move mountains. Without passion, you can be talented, and certainly talent has something to do with special physical gifts, but these are no guarantee of success later on.

> "Secretly, we are all volcanoes, and if we are denied the opportunity to release our excess emotional power ... well then, some people suddenly and unexpectedly erupt. Because dance is the natural release for all human impulses, for anger, for pain, for joy, warning or friendship."
>
> Anna Pavlova

When I remember my childhood, my swaybacked legs, my little apple-like bottom and my almost complete lack of turn-out, anyone who looked at me must have thought: dance is not really for her. Even my brother had better physical attributes than I did. He could easily do so many of the exercises that I really had to struggle at with clenched teeth. But he didn't have the dream, nor did he feel that passion for ballet.

My first pointe shoes

I will never forget my childhood memories. I was just nine years old. I went with my father to the magnificent Deutsche Staatsoper Unter den Linden to see a performance of *Invitation To The Dance*, in which students of the National Ballet School in Berlin were also appearing. At that time I had already been in a children's dance group for three years, and danced, filled with passion and delight, both in the ballet studio and in the children's performances. However, what I was to see on that particular evening on the stage of the Staatsoper was to change my future and my life.

The skill of the students and dancers in this ballet, the beautiful costumes, the pointe shoes in which even twelve-year-old girls were already allowed to dance, the whole sparkling atmosphere on the stage and in the theatre made such an impression on me that I wanted to learn this profession. More than anything else in the world, I longed to be able to dance, myself, as a ballerina on this great stage.

However in those days, my passion for the profession was to be sorely tried, as first of all I had to get through several exams. After passing the screening and aptitude test, I would have a whole year to wait, before I would be allowed to take part in the real audition. I passed, and at last I became a real ballet student. The longed-for realisation of my childhood dream had made its tentative start.

Of course I wanted to get up on pointe as soon as I could. Unfortunately, mastering the art of dancing didn't go as quickly and as smoothly as I had imagined at first. Learning how to dance on pointe took me a lot of time, and required not only strength and determination, but above all the necessary patience. I waited, filled with longing, for my teacher finally to give me some pointe shoes. However, first of all my feet needed to be strengthened before I was allowed to work on pointe.

Then at last, after half a year of training, I was given my first pointe shoes. How often I had dreamed of this moment, and now it had finally become a reality. I was given some Russian shoes, at least a size smaller than my normal shoe size. Just to hold the tiny pair in my hands, to smell them and touch them, filled me with incredible happiness.

When I was considered ready for the shoes, when I slipped them on and felt them on my feet, then rose for the first time onto pointe, it was the greatest moment of my life. I could already see myself as a famous ballerina, enchanting the public in the most beautiful costumes. In my mind I could even feel the make-up and smell the stage.

And then during my first year of training, I found myself once again at the Deutschen Staatsoper Unter den Linden. Only this time, I was on the other side of the curtain. Now, I was one of the ballet students in the Ballet *Invitation To The Dance*, and shortly before the red curtain closed for the last time, our row of girls was allowed for the briefest moment to go up onto our pointes.

The toothmug

Plastic toothmugs had to serve as my first actual "pointe shoes", while I was still at kindergarten. This was not without risk, as my feet were still very small, and my ankles weak. But I loved to squeeze my feet into their firm grip, get myself up off the floor and prance about all over the place. I wanted to be a ballerina too, like the ones I had seen in pictures or on television. Much later I heard from lots of dancers, that they too in their childhood had tried out these unconventional "pointe shoes".

However the reality of everyday school life quickly brought me back down to earth. I found it hard to become "weightless", to master the technique, to glide effortlessly over the floor. But I refused to become discouraged. It took a few more years of hard, sweaty work, before at last I actually reached that wonderful moment of "lift-off".

During my seven years of training I learned, not least through intense and trusting collaboration with my teachers, to cope with success and failure, both as a student and later on as a professional. I learned that I did not need to accept every limitation of my body and my spirit, that I could treat them as challenges, as markers along the way to my chosen objective: to one day become a real ballerina!

Your first pointe shoes?

Maybe you're holding a pair of pointe shoes in your hand for the first time, or you want to go into the dancewear shop and try some on. Then let me explain a couple of things to you.

The shoes are going to seem very hard and stiff, like a bone. They're going to feel very uncomfortable, and probably squeeze you all over your foot. But don't let this first impression scare you off. The pointe shoes are still in their so-called "raw" stage. Now it's up to you to tailor them to your own needs. Don't become so awestruck by the beauty of the shoes that you find yourself putting up with perfectly avoidable physical discomfort.

You have to know that the shoe is only waiting for you to work on it. For example all you need to do is gently to bend the sole and soften the box a little by kneading it with your fingers, and the shoe will already feel different on your foot. You'll see that with a couple of little tricks and techniques which you can find in this book, you can get a totally different feeling from dancing and working with your pointe shoes.

"For the gymnast, the movement and culture of the body are an end in themselves, but for the dance they are only the means. The body itself must then be forgotten; it is only an instrument harmonised, and well appropriated, and its movements do not express, as in gymnastics, only the movements of a body, but, through that body, they express also the sentiments and thoughts of the soul."

Isadora Duncan

Your first steps on pointe?

Now you're certain. You definitely want to learn how to dance on pointe, the way the great ballerinas do. And you can see no reason why you shouldn't try it out. Of course you can do so, but don't try to do it alone. Put your trust in your teachers, and in people who really have experience of dancing on pointe.

However, before you start to work on pointe, you have to know that your feet, toes and ankles will need to be strengthened by means of specially-designed exercises. This is very important, to avoid injuring yourself and to be certain that dancing on pointe will continue to give you pleasure. Your beautiful dance dream mustn't be shattered forever because of a damaged foot. Your dance teacher will prepare you carefully, and advise you.

Initially, of course, dancing with pointe shoes on will feel strange and unaccustomed. Nonetheless, if your passionate determination persists, you are sure to master the art of pointe work quite soon.

Did you know

that it can often take years to find your "own" pointe shoes? A race against time, when you think how short a dancer's career is. But now, you've got this book!

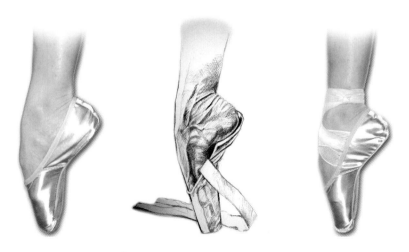

WORTH KNOWING

In the Rococo ballets of the early 18th century, the dancers used to wear courtly shoes with block heels. A famous dancer at the French court, Marie Camargo (1710–1770), was the first to remove these heels, so as to allow as much technical virtuosity in her male rôles as possible. However she still didn't actually dance on pointe.

The first recorded instances of pointe work are to be found at the end of the 18th and the beginning of the 19th centuries. The world of literature and of the theatre was at that stage completely enchanted by tales of shepherds, elves, dryads, nymphs and fairies. The lyrical, the marvellous and the magical were suddenly seen by artists as the true inspiration for their interpretations.

The Italian ballet-master and choreographer, Carlo Blasis (1797–1878), whose theories constituted the beginning of academic classical ballet, is said to have invented the pointe shoe. In his classes he laid great stress on the development of pointe technique, as long as fifteen years before the general acceptance of pointe shoes onstage.

Did you know

that uninformed spectators often see the pointe shoe only as a part of the costume? For the dancer, however, the pointe shoe is as essential as the violin is to a violinist. And just like the violin, the pointe shoe must be looked after and tuned, to bring it to its full potential as an instrument.

At the performance of the romantic ballet *La Sylphide* in 1832 in Paris an enthusiastic audience was able for the first time to experience the perfected pointe-work of the Italian ballerina Marie Taglioni (1804–1884). Her father, Filippo Taglioni (1777–1871), was the first choreographer to use pointe technique as a means of lyrical expression, thereby lending it artistic acceptability. It was now no longer about celebrating the ability to pull off technical stunts on pointe. When the ballerina rose onto the tips of her toes, she was transformed for the rapturous audience into an ethereal being, who seemed able to float effortlessly through space and time. With Taglioni a new tradition came to life: the romantic ballet.

Ever since, the newly-born dance on pointe has excited the imaginations of choreographers and librettists. They introduced new technique and content into their ballets.

Dance on pointe became gradually more refined and technically better, with the advent of constantly improved shoes. Italian shoemakers are said to have been the first to add support to the toe-block of the light Atlas shoe (a pretty cloth shoe) so that their dancers could stay up on pointe for longer, and execute unusual combinations of pirouettes and steps.

Some ballerinas who managed really to master the pointe technique and above all to bring it to life, enjoyed worldwide success. Beside the ethereally sensuous Taglioni, there were the lyrical-dramatic Carlotta Grisi (1819–1899), the lively and enchanting Fanny Cerrito (1817–1909) and the powerful, romantic Lucile Grahn (1819–1907).

Did you know

that some of the fans of the ballerina Taglioni were once so enraptured that after a farewell performance in St. Petersburg, they cooked and ate a pair of her pointe shoes?

Even if the flower of the romantic period in choreography did not last long, certain famous works of this period are still maintained and kept alive even today, ballets such as *La Sylphide*, *Pas de quatre* – this piece was especially made for the four ballerinas listed above – or *Giselle*, the dream ballet of every ballerina. The special appeal of these ballets, their dreamlike beauty and elegance, will probably continue to fascinate audiences for a long time.

Dancing on pointe developed further towards the end of the 19th century. This was a period when many of the great classical ballets were made. The French ballet-master and choreographer Marius Petipa (1818–1910) created masterpieces that even today form part of the repertoire of many of the great classical companies: *Don Quixote, La Bayadère* and *The Sleeping Beauty*. Together with Lev Ivanov (1834-1901) he created the famous *Swan Lake*. With these ballets, Petipa created a brilliant, virtuoso style that required perfect mastery of pointe technique from the dancers. Even today, generations later, the technical and artistic ability of a ballerina is measured and judged by her performance of these rôles.

Did you know

that George Balanchine, one of the most famous choreographers of the 20th century, is reputed once to have said that he would never have begun to choreograph if the pointe shoe had not been invented?

Yet another outstanding pointe artist also requires mention at this point, the legendary Anna Pavlova (1881–1931). She went down in ballet history, above all for her interpretation of the *Dying Swan* solo, choreographed by Michael Fokine (1880-1942). An art critic is reported to have said of her, "The soul of the dance has taken shape in Pavlova".

Even today, the art of dancing on pointe has lost none of its popularity with the public and with dancers, despite the fact that modern dance and all sorts of different styles, with and without pointe shoes, have now found their way into the world of ballet.

Pointe shoe – how you've changed!

The pointe shoes of Taglioni can still be seen today in the library of the Paris Opera. There are also pointe shoes worn and signed by Lucile Grahn in the German Dance Archives in Cologne, and they are impressive, not only because of their age. If you compare these pointe shoes with the shoes of today, you will be amazed most of all by their softness. In those days, they were only slightly reinforced in the block, and the sole, so that the first ballerinas to dance on pointe can only really have been able to stay up for very short periods of time.

Pointe shoes today, on the other hand, are much more elaborately constructed. They support the dancer's foot much better, and offer more stability when dancing. Even so, every dancer still has to conquer these shoes, by dint of much hard work and effort.

The picture shows German pointe shoes, as they were still being made in 1970 by the theatre cobbler at the Deutsche Staatsoper Unter den Linden in Berlin. You can see in the picture that the pointes and the block have been slightly reinforced for the front part of the foot. These shoes, too, were used in the execution of virtuoso technique. When I tried them on, I was horrified and at the same time amazed, at what the feet of the dancers must have gone through in these extremely outdated pointe shoes. It would have been sheer torture for me to have to dance in them. To me they felt much too narrow in the block, and much too unyielding in the sole. Maybe the narrow pointe shoes would have been popular with dancers because they made the feet look particularly graceful and dainty.

Very soon, pointe shoes were being adapted to the changed requirements of today's dancers. Perhaps for the first time on medical grounds, the block area was now built deeper and broader. The block was more elaborately constructed, and the reinforced layers formed and moulded to support the arch of the foot and distribute the body weight so as to spare the ankles. If you compare the pictures, you can see this at once.

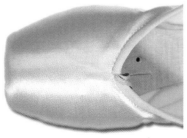

Men and pointe work?

Until recently, dancing on pointe has been the preserve of women. More and more, though, male dancers are daring to try out pointe work. And in fact today, increasing numbers of choreographers are discovering and using pointe technique as a new means of expression for men as well, for character rôles in classical ballets and in modern dance pieces.

A friend of mine, a French choreographer, told me that when he was training to be a dancer, all the boys in his school had to do pointe classes, and that some schools teach this technique even today. This was to strengthen the feet and develop their footwork. The boys learned at first hand how much time and patience is required to perfect the working of the instrument. Having experienced this on their own feet they had a much better appreciation of the problems and needs of the girls in their school. They became much more considerate, especially in those delicate moments when the dancer once again has to wait, while his partner fidgets and tinkers endlessly with her shoes.

He personally found that this experience later helped him to become a much better partner in pas de deux work, because he could understand the problems better. It also helps him now, as a choreographer, to create steps on pointe.

I'm sure you've also heard of *Les Ballets Trockadero de Monte Carlo*, a ballet company that consists entirely of men. These male dancers have dedicated themselves completely to the art of the ballerina. Certainly it must have been funny in the beginning, with men dancing on pointe and performing women's rôles.

These men tour all over the world, with ballets from the classical repertoire in which they dance all of the female rôles with the original choreography, and they have had and are still enjoying tremendous success.

"A ballet is a movement in time and space, a living instant. Like a hothouse flower it blooms, then dies. A ballet is life. It is not a monument or a column, standing there for ever, nor a painting, but something that belongs to the people who perform it, to their bodies."

George Balanchine

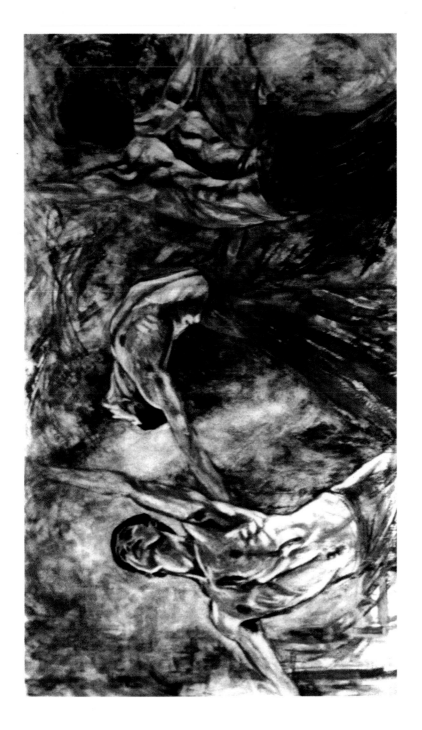

TOO MANY CHOICES

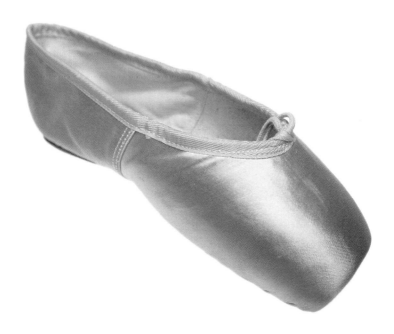

The "perfect" pointe shoe

Who among us is not searching for it – the ideal pointe shoe which fits perfectly at once, doesn't pinch in the block, isn't too wide at the sides, has enough flexibility in the sole, holds your foot firmly and securely, lasts a long time and also makes your foot look wonderful, in other words wins you over completely? A shoe which, even despite the generous platform of the block, is not too wide, so that the front of the foot doesn't collapse and the big toe doesn't get too much floor pressure, so that the weight on the toes is evenly distributed? That's what everyone wants, and shoes that can fulfil all these wishes aren't necessarily ready and waiting in the shops.

Apart from giving me pain in the feet, wrong, unfinished or twisted shoes make me feel physically ill, to the point where I develop a real knot in the pit of my stomach. Completely impossible to dance in. I rip these shoes off my feet and throw them into the nearest corner. With some shoes I know that even after I've worked on them, I will never become fond of them. However that doesn't mean that every shoe which feels uncomfortable the first time must immediately be got rid of.

My pointe shoe = your pointe shoe?

You can't always see that pointe shoes vary one from another, but even so, there are differences in the sole and the block, in their stiffness and durability. Even shoes made on a production line vary from one pair to the next, although they're the same model. That's why, if you've forgotten your shoes for a performance or a rehearsal, you can't easily replace them with someone else's. Every dancer spends an awful lot of time trying on, adapting and working on her own personal shoes, to be able to dance with them as well as she possibly can. Quite apart from the question of size, the characteristics of feet are so specific to their owners, that you can hardly find one single dancer whose shoes are "tuned" exactly the same way as your own. In any case, the substitution will certainly affect the way you feel, and have a perceptible effect on the technical and artistic quality of your work.

My foot = your foot?

Every foot is different as well, so every foot needs a special pointe shoe. The feet in the picture above actually look nearly identical. Even so, they are different. Because, despite having the same shoe size and more or less similar characteristics, the dancer on the left needs a shoe with a high, broad box and a stronger sole for her foot, because she has a very good arch. The other girl, in contrast, prefers a narrower pointe shoe with a more pliable sole, as her arch is less pronounced.

Choosing pointe shoes

As a beginner, you should never order reserve supplies of pointe shoes in large quantities, because it would only be by the greatest possible good luck that your first shoes would also turn out to be the best ones for you. Anyway, this way you can also quickly and easily try out different models or other makers. First considerations when making your choice should be size, form and the characteristics of the pointe shoe, later on, when dancing, their wearing comfort and durability!

While writing this book, I have consciously refrained from passing judgement on any particular type of foot, maker or special design. Because these factors are so complex, and so important for your health and your development as a dancer, you should get personal advice from teachers and specialists! Take time together! Look carefully at the shape of your foot! The deciding factors are above all the length of the toes, their size in relation to each other, the breadth and length of your metatarsal region, the height of your instep, the transverse arch and other such considerations. Your condition and the level of dance technique which you have reached are also of great significance.

Choose your shoes on this basis, with a specific degree of hardness, height and length of vamp, appropriate strength of sole, size of platform, heel height and other features.

The best thing is to try your pointe shoes on bare feet, or if necessary in the shop, with nylon socks. Although of course if you want to wear cotton socks, block inlays or toe protectors later, you'll need to wear these when trying on your pointe shoes. The shoe mustn't be too big, otherwise it becomes difficult to work with and control. This is really not a moment for your parents to try to save money, because they think you're still growing. Contrary to the prevailing generally accepted idea of the layman, dancing on pointe is not strictly speaking "toe dancing". A dancer on pointe stands on the entire stretched forefoot, and the load is evenly distributed by a good pointe shoe on and around the metatarsal area and over the sole.

Did you know

that the life of a pair of pointe shoes is really very short? In order to lengthen it a little, sometimes only minimal corrections or the use of the right glue can be enough to allow the pair to be re-used. Have a look in "Tips & Tricks".

If the shoe is too big, you'll be able to recognise this because your toes are going to have too much room in the block, and you really will be standing on the tips of your toes. But also, your foot can slide about here and there inside the shoe, or the back seam slips down too easily off your heel.

If, however, your pointe shoes are too small, you will also notice this very quickly. They will really squeeze your foot together, causing the toes to bend excessively and leaving them no space to lie side by side. The block is simply too tight.

Your shoes fit properly when your metatarsus doesn't slide down in the shoe, but is supported by the sides of the block. Your toes are only lightly touching the ends of the shoe, and the back seam doesn't immediately slither off your foot when you are on demi-pointe (half-pointe). These shoes would be suitable for you to work on. You have to know that pointe shoes warm up during dancing, and because of heat, movement and sweat, they will stretch a little.

Left or Right?

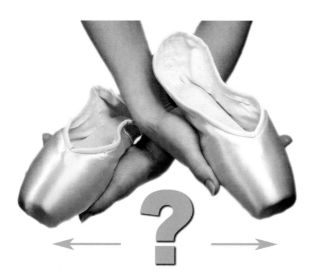

Generally, in the case of unmodified pairs of pointe shoes, both shoes are the same. During the trying on of shoes, the dancer's feet decide which one should be the right shoe and which the left. Finally the shoes will differ one from the other when the ribbons are attached.

Listen to your foot!

When you look at this picture for the first time, you may not immediately notice that these are actually several different makes of pointe shoe. Even a really experienced eye will have to look more than once to discern the minute differences in design and construction. It's only when you first try them on that the foot can really form an impression of each shoe.

In the dancewear shops you can find a great many varying pointe shoe models from different pointe shoe suppliers. Some of them are particularly suitable for beginners, while others are better suited to experienced dancers. The cheapest shoes will not necessarily turn out to be the best buy. Sometimes expensive shoes last a lot longer, and are therefore easier on your piggy-bank or the wallets of your parents. High price alone, however, is a far cry from a guarantee of durability.

Above all, listen to your foot! Give it a try! And after some time, you will find you have made a preliminary or maybe a permanent decision in favour of one make of pointe shoe. When eventually the shoe no longer feels like a ball and chain, when it has become, so to speak, a second skin for you, then the technique of mastering the shoe can slowly recede into the background. Then you'll be able to abandon yourself entirely to portraying the rôle, to dancing.

Did you know

that reworking your own pointe shoes is also somehow like labouring on a little work of art? So many thoughts, so much psychic energy and awareness are poured into this shoe during the tuning process. Sometimes while working on a pair of shoes, I've danced all the way through entire performances in my head.

Of course manufacturers are aware that a dancer has high expectations of her shoes. Each firm tries hard to make the best shoes for the dancers, and to offer a wide range of sizes, breadths and firmness. For decades they have been fiddling about, together with dancers and orthopaedic surgeons, to find a special shoe that lets the foot dance by itself. A very difficult undertaking, one realises, bearing in mind how many differing feet there are, each one craving for its own, individually-adapted shoe.

Did you know

that some pointe shoe suppliers offer the same shoe in varying forms? They are sold with loose or even sewn-on ribbons and elastics, with a leather block cover already glued on or merely enclosed. If you happen to have enough pointe shoe ribbons already, you could always use the extras for hair-ribbons or to pretty up presents that you want to give.

Recently-developed pointe shoes, in contrast to the usual models, are padded even in the block, the entire sole and in the heel area, so as to render the shoe as comfortable as possible for the dancer. These pointe shoes are said to last a lot longer and place less of a strain on the ankles, thanks to their improved characteristics and materials. They are, of course, remarkably expensive.

However, established dancers in particular often seem to find it very difficult to accept a new make of shoe. For one thing they have become accustomed to the qualities but also the imperfections of their own pointe shoe model, and for another many dancers prefer an unsprung contact with the floor, and therefore find the extra padding a distraction.

Beginners or prospective dancers should not become involved in trying out these novelties. Just as, in cooking, only the palate can really judge matters of taste and food quality, so when choosing pointe shoes, it is above all the dancer's foot that can feel the quality of a shoe and make the final choice.

Look out for the signs!

Pointe shoes come in different sizes, widths and strengths, for example in S, M, W, or else X, XX, XXX, XXXX. All the distinguishing marks are different, not only between varying brands but even within the same range of models of one brand with different makers!

Assuming you have now found your brand of pointe shoe, make sure that when ordering or buying your shoes, you can identify them by the sign and number on the back of the sole, which identify their maker.

Each maker has his own style and many of the 100 or so work processes are still carried out by hand. Thus it may well happen that the shoe you have ordered arrives with another maker's mark on it, and for you it feels like a totally different shoe on your foot, simply because this time it was made by the maker at the neighbouring last.

Maybe this maker uses a little more glue in the block, to hold the materials together, or he left the shoe a little longer in the oven to dry. Perhaps its just the different soul of this new maker than makes the subtle difference.

So be careful! Otherwise the shoe or the order will have to be sent back, which unfortunately costs time and probably also your money.

Branded marks on the outer sole of different pointe shoes.

Secondhand?

As a Principal Dancer, I used to get through a lot of pointe shoes. Twelve to twenty pairs a month was by no means unusual for me, and also among the other soloists. Sometimes for a *Swan Lake* I would use up two to three pairs of shoes; for another particular production as many as five pairs, because they were dyed to fit different costumes. The management of the ballet company used to be very upset by the numerous bills from pointe shoe makers.

Did you know

that discarded pairs of pointe shoes from the dancers, usually of the bigger theatres, are sometimes collected for use by the students of the ballet schools? It's certainly worth finding out about; then maybe not every pair will have to be bought brand new from the shop.

I spent many hours a week working on and adjusting my pointe shoes. One of my colleagues, who used to have great problems in finding and adjusting her pointe shoes, came up with an unusual idea. She tried out my used pointe shoes, in the hope that they might fit her. She was delighted to find that these used shoes were ideal for her needs. She used to tidy them up and modify them a little, then she was able to dance with them almost immediately. Now she didn't need to darn and break in each pair of new pointe shoes, which saved her a lot of time.

And my high consumption of pointe shoes was easier for the ballet management to accept, because the same shoes were now being used twice. My colleague was happy, and the directors saved a lot of money.

Although this sort of thing is not usual for most dancers, there are in fact some people who use this alternative. Be careful, though! Before you try out the used shoes of a friend or a colleague, you need a lot of experience in the requirements of your particular foot. Saving money should never be the sole basis for this kind of decision.

IN THE POINTE SHOE WORKSHOP

The rolls of ribbon pictured above remind me of my first ballet shoes. Together with my children's dance teacher, I visited a theatre shoemaker to find a pair for myself. My eyes were as wide as saucers. All these rolls of pink shoe ribbon, great heaps of ballet slippers, pointe shoes and other stage and costume shoes. There was a powerful smell of glue, wood and leather.

A new world opened before me in that little room. The smell of the theatre! A workshop for stage magic and transformation. My imagination was turning somersaults. I could happily have stayed there for ever. When I finally had to leave, I took this fascination home with me, and hoped that some day I might again be able to buy my ballet slippers in this very special shoemaker's. At that stage I had no idea that later on in my life I would be in and out of many such workshops.

For many years I searched for "my" pointe shoe. During this period I went through several stages of believing that I had finally found the right shoe for me. But I was forced to realise that my feet, which were subject to heavy demands, were slowly but surely changing! Especially when I stopped training for a bit while I was having my baby, my feet took advantage of the opportunity to spread themselves out.

Indeed, after that I literally needed a pointe shoe that was a whole size larger than before. Also my feet reacted more intensely to the alternating periods of rest and stress, or to different weather conditions with their very own ebb and flood tides. As I was also being challenged by a series of minor injuries, I came at last to the conclusion that I was going to have to go through the whole question of the fit, size and condition of my working tools all over again.

So once more, I went to see my shoemaker at the Deutsche Staatsoper Unter den Linden in Berlin. Together we decided not to change the shoe-last of another dancer, which had been re-built years ago to my measurements, but instead to build a whole new pointe shoe last, just for me.

A last of your own!

What a luxury for a dancer – made-to-measure pointe shoes! Not every dancer gets to enjoy such a pleasure during her career. Except, perhaps, those who can afford it privately.

The shoemaker then made a couple of pairs of the new model for me to try out. That way we were able to keep the losses to a minimum, in case the shoes were for some reason or another not quite right. We kept on changing and modifying until we were satisfied with the results. So I was in constant contact with the shoemaker, who became an important partner in my dancing career.

I often asked myself why, even now that I had my own last, there was never a pair of pointe shoes that were completely ready for me and needed no adjustment. But, as I have already said, even one's own shoemaker doesn't work exactly the same every day. It's like baking a cake – it never comes out exactly the same twice in a row. Also, I have much more faith in my shoes when I have previously held them in my hand, modified them and got to know them. Each new pair is different, and each pair is always a new challenge.

What is a pointe shoe made of?

Pointe shoe manufacturers use many different materials, and the production of a shoe requires more than 100 stages. So much time and work! In fact, it's true to say that a pointe shoe is a real work of art. It's a pity it gets used up so quickly. Every manufacturer has his own secret "recipe". Most of the time, the secret in shoe construction is in the composition of the glue, and also in the combination of the materials used, which then give the shoe the special qualities of resilience, elasticity, hardness and durability that characterise each brand.

In the picture above you can see the materials which are required for the manufacture of pointe shoes. Among them are rough and smooth leather, linen, satin and a mixture of papier-mâché and leather. The necessary production materials are fastened to the last, which we have already encountered, repeatedly pulled onto it, wrapped round it and glued together. To harden them, the shoes will eventually spend many hours in the oven at a temperature of around 70° C. In the lower picture you can see uppers from the cover and the back seam. These are basically the total material covering of the pointe shoe. They are pre-assembled inside out, fastened to the last and then further manipulated.

Anatomy of a pointe shoe

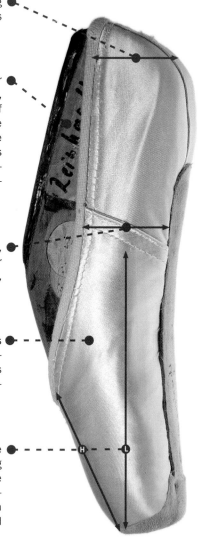

The heel may often be of varying heights, depending on the dancer's needs in this area.

The last is made of wood, plastic or artificial resin, either in standard sizes, or else according to the dimensions of a dancer's foot. Particular stages in the shoe's construction determine shape and size. When a shoe is ready, it is again pulled onto the last and hammered, to remove accidental irregularities in the block.

The side-pieces are of varying heights, according to the "cut" of the particular model of shoe, the width of the block, and the wings.

The material of **the outer covering** is usually satin. This material is very hard-wearing and dirt-repellent, and comes in various different colours. It is attached to an interior lining of linen.

The front section is the front part of the shoe, as far as the waist-seam, including the vamp. The length and height of the material are adapted to the characteristics of the dancer's foot, depending on length, the width of the metatarsus and the strength of the instep.

The **drawstring** casing contains the drawstring, and is sewn to the shoe. Often an elastic or cloth string is pulled through, so as to be able to fasten the shoe as well as possible.

The **outer sole**, usually of leather, is attached to the material, the shank and the insole. It is first sewn, then attached with tacks or small nails.

The **insole** consists of a material-covered complete sole. In this model it is made of a compressed leather-based material.

The **shank** is also known as the "backbone" of the shoe, and is made up of layers of various materials. In this picture it is made of red vulcanised fibre. The stiffness of the shoe is chosen according to each dancer's foot.

The **block, or toe-box** is made up of various layer of coarse linen, held together with a mixture of papier-mâché and leather, and potato starch. The vamp and the wing come in varying heights and widths.

The **point, or platform**, is the level surface on which the foot stands when on pointe.

"Passion and Desire"

TIPS & TRICKS

In this chapter I want to offer you some suggestions on how with a couple of tricks you can improve the interaction between foot and shoe in a short time. It should be possible for you to create a pointe shoe which is attuned to the requirements of your foot, which achieves the best possible conditions when you are dancing, and which offers you security and flexibility at the same time. From now on, uncomfortable shoes no longer have to wind up in the rubbish bin. One just needs to know how to deal with them.

Bear in mind that quite often for some problems there are various different solutions you can try. Don't try all of them at once, just choose one of them, and then as you go along, you can decide which solution seems best to you.

One thing is sure; you won't be able to solve all of your problems immediately. You also need to be clever with your hands for some of these jobs, but this will improve, the more you practise. Don't despair, you'll see that very soon you will be making progress, and gathering sufficient experience.

Poor shoemaker

My shoemakers were often taken aback and in some cases astounded when I showed some of them how I used to dismember the pointe shoes which they had so lovingly shaped and built. If they only knew how, in the privacy of the dressing room, the shoes were pounded, cut, broken, stabbed and torn! Some of the shoemakers were horrified at the sight.

Worrying about making the first incision

Oh, what a beautiful shiny new pointe shoe! You just want to embrace it constantly and gaze at it all the time, it looks so perfect and unflawed. The firmness of the shape, the silky smoothness of the material, the smell of it, the ornate brand mark on the sole.

No! You can't do anything violent to this shoe!!!

Now let's get one thing clear. It's got to be either you or the shoe! As I've already explained, the perfection of a pointe shoe is not only defined by its superficial, unused appearance. It is a tool that is meant to be at your service, not the other way around. You shouldn't let your misplaced reverence for the beauty of the pointe shoe stop you from improving it. Because whatever you don't do to this shoe, your feet will have to pay the price for it. And a new foot is something you can't buy just like that in the shops.

Even after you've adapted them, the pointe shoes on your feet can still look very beautiful onstage, and sometimes they even owe this beauty to your modifications. Also as time goes by you will become cleverer and quicker at using your working materials. Think about yourself! When you get onstage, it's not pointe shoes you want to present, but yourself and your own charisma as a dancer.

Did you know

that to make a pair of pointe shoes "stage-ready" means to prepare them especially for your coming performance? Most of the time several pairs will be prepared and broken in for a show, before on the day of the performance, one or two pairs make the short-list. Sometimes it's even shortly before the performance that the final decision is made over which pointe shoes are the best for this evening and these feet. For rehearsals, on the other hand, one doesn't need to spend quite so much time on the choice.

"Well-done"

When you become a dancer, you'll find that the pointe shoes you use for rehearsals and performances haven't got to be the most beautiful ones any longer. For professional dancers, comfortable class shoes are the main consideration. After they've been used for performances or important rehearsals, shoes are often worn for a long time.

You can see what these ex-pointe shoes look like in the photograph above. After their duty onstage was finished, I cannibalised them, and for a long time I used them in class as "flatties" (see the chapter on "Soft shoes").

Did you know

that old ballet flatties or pointe shoes are often known as "slippers" when they start to look too comfortable and floppy? Most of the time they really are worn-out, and no longer correspond to the aesthetic image of beautiful, clean ballet shoes.

Your tools

Generally speaking for the job of modifying your pointe shoes you will need very good sewing and working implements, and of course two strong, nimble hands.

- Sewing needles of different strengths, a thimble or a thin leather glove, so as not to stab yourself through the fingers.

- A wide mallet for pounding and softening the block.

- Scissors: one pair of small pointed ones and one large pair for cutting and getting rid of material.

- A scraper for the sole of the shoe.

- A medium-sized screwdriver for levering out staples or nails.

- Pincers or pliers for pulling out shoe-tacks. I use an old carpenter's nail-puller.

- Yarn: cotton thread, twine and darning cotton.

More haste, less speed!

Sometimes when I was working, the needle didn't manage to get through the shoe, but did stab me in the hand. Experience showed that lots of little bloodstains all over the shoe produced unwanted patterns like the spots on a fly agaric mushroom. So what did this teach me? Take your time over the re-working of the shoes, so that you work with a calm, steady hand, and make sure you're using good tools.

Your yarn

Use cotton yarn to sew your shoes with. It is available in different strengths and calibres (thin or thick yarn).

If possible, it should not fuzz. You can tell, if you pull back lightly on the yarn, whether it has been spun tight or loose. When you're doing this, the yarn should not immediately separate into several different threads, otherwise it will disintegrate under the strain of the job it has to do.

Yarn that is too thin or too tight also cuts your skin. Even so, it's alright for use in sewing jobs on the side of the shoe.

Tuning the pointe shoe

On the following pages I have put together for you a number of questions and problems, with various solutions which could certainly prove very useful. If you're not so experienced with pointe shoes, then talk through each alteration with your teachers. First of all, have a look through all the tips in peace and quiet. Maybe you'll find the answer to a problem you thought was insoluble. Each of the blue points marks the beginning of a new tip.

Pointe – platform – base

1. The platform is too slippery?

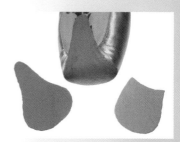

● You can rub crushed resin (a special material which musicians use for their violin bows) into the platform. Or else keep a damp cloth in the wings to moisten the platforms (see item 10).

● You can also glue a leather cover onto the platform. Ready-made toe-caps can be bought in dancewear shops (as in the photograph above).

● Or you can remove the covering from the platform by cutting round it. If you don't want to darn the entire pointe, there are some makes of shoes which will require you to cut back all the material under the platform, right back as far as the sole, so that it doesn't fray.

● If you've already got a leather toe-cap, you can roughen it up with the points of the scissors or something similar. You can also pierce small holes in the leather.

● Or you can score and scratch the surface. This way the resin will stick better and last longer.

2. The platform is too small, too slippery or too soft?

Sew all the way round the platform, as shown in the picture. If you're using shoes without toe-caps, sew round the platform as shown in the picture below.

Sewing technique for pointe shoes:

Use a big, thick needle for this, with double thread and a thimble. First, if the platform of the shoe hasn't got a leather toe-cap, you can remove the satin, as in item 1. Start at the side of the pointe shoe, using stitches there with no knots, which tend to distract the eye and cause pressure on the foot.

With each stitch, lead the yarn through the loop of the previous stitch (blanket-stitch technique).

When you come back on the next row, stitch diagonally into this seam, (this time without loops). Using a vertical stitch is also an option.

At the end, stitch the yarn into the seam, again without knots, so that it disappears into the earlier stitches.

If the pointe is too soft, pour or brush on a little pointe shoe glue with Pointe Hardener or shellac inside the shoe. This method won't work on shoes with blocks or soles of synthetic material, which can't absorb the shellac.

You can use transparent nail varnish for smaller places (see item 16, Tip 2).

3. When on pointe does the shoe stand crooked, possibly through wear and tear?

Even out the differences in height by repeated darning, using the technique detailed under item 2, only this time sewing back and forth several times. What you are doing is building up a small raised area, which removes the crookedness (see item 14, Tip 1).

4. The shoe is too loud, or too hard?

Take a wooden mallet to the platform or the block, and hammer it soft.

Hit the shoe hard on the floor several times (see the chapter "The block – the wing").

You can also darn the pointe as described under item 2, which helps to make it quieter.

The block – the wing

5. The block is too hard?

Hammer the block soft with a wide hammer or mallet, or something similar. Sometimes it's enough just to use the other pointe shoe.

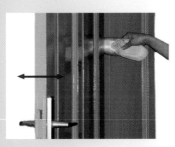

Squeeze the block in the hinge space between a door and its frame, moving the door carefully back and forth. Be careful of your fingers!

Moisten the block inside and out with water. You can also do this with wet hands. The block will mould itself better to your foot.

Hold the block in a jet of steam, so as to soften the glue. Don't scald either yourself or the shoe! When it's cooled down enough, knead the block with your fingers and put on the still-damp shoe. Leave it on for a few minutes.

6. The block is too wide or too narrow, or the foot needs varying block widths because it tends to swell and then contract, or you need more support for your instep?

The following sewing technique for linking the side parts allows you to open and close the vamp.

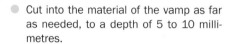

Cut into the material of the vamp as far as needed, to a depth of 5 to 10 millimetres.

If necessary, remove superfluous material in a wedge shape around the cut. When the sides are joined this will give you a better line.

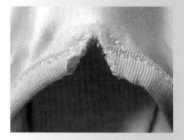

Some models have a drawstring threaded through a drawstring casing, which you can remove.

Now sew the sides together, starting from the centre of the cut-out vamp, without knots, and using a firm, non-fraying cotton yarn.

Sew the yarn in a zigzag pattern, like the laces on normal shoes, except that in this case you have only one lace, the length of which you can adjust as required.

How far across the instep you need to use this technique for support is something you will simply have to find out by trial and error.

Anchor the yarn firmly to the inside of the shoe, using a special loop (no knots!).

You can undo this loop easily, tighten and re-tie it. Then hide the spare end of yarn inside the shoe.

You can also use this shoelace to increase support for your instep, even without cutting into the shoe.

Another method is to sew wide, firm elastic to the interior of the sides of the vamp (see also items 37 and 38).

7. Are you looking for a way to relieve the pain from blisters, among other things?

- Cut a small hole in the block, to decrease the pressure on the blister.

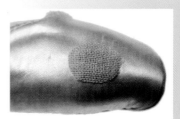

Cover the hole from outside with a bandage.

Once you've disguised the bandage with make-up and coloured it over, it will be practically invisible (see the chapters on "Foot Hygiene" and "Granny's special recipes").

The sole – outer

8. Half-point (demi-pointe) is not really satisfactorily possible, the shoe is not pliable enough?

Bend the new shoe carefully back and forth. If you sense that it is resisting, you can if necessary use a little more force. Try the shoe on every now and then, though, to see if it has already reached your required degree of suppleness (see items 13 and 14).

Score the sole with scissors or something equivalent, in horizontal and slightly wedge-shaped lines.

These cuts make the shoe more flexible. Some dancers even completely remove the outer sole. This, however, is only recommended when training is completed.

9. The sole is too slippery or too uneven?

Roughen or scratch off the thin, slippery top layer from the sole, using scissors for example, or remove these uneven areas from the sole.

You can also buy special pointe shoe scrapers in dancewear shops.

10. The pointe shoes are too slippery for use on parquet or similar surfaces?

● Using special glue, fasten a thin layer of leather (possibly even non-slip leather as used on ordinary street shoes) over the pointe. You can also have this done by a normal shoe repair shop (see item 1).

11. The use of resin is not allowed, or else there is none available?

● Moisten the shoe with water, if necessary with sugared water, lemonade or cola (lightly diluted with water) or have the floor washed with it. First of all, try out the strength of the dilution on a small surface. If there's too much sugar in the mixture, there's a danger that it will become squeaky and really sticky. A bucket of warm water with a couple of squirts of ammonia in it is also said to be good when cleaning slippery floors.

Did you know

that every new stage floor feels strange at first, and therefore needs to be conquered again with pointe shoes? Only dancers can really understand how much seemingly minor differences from one floor to the next will affect their dancing. Sometimes the floor is harder, not as resilient as before, sometimes it feels somewhat softer than you are accustomed to. You have the feeling of sinking into it. Sometimes it's more slippery, then again sometimes duller.

The sole — inner

12. The material of the inner sole is too slippery?

Remove the material of the inner sole, or cut it in half. You may need to glue the edges of the sole, so that it doesn't roll up when you dance.

Moisten the material of the sole or the sole of your tights with water before use.

Or rub some resin into the inner sole and heel of the pointe shoe and the heel of your tights.

13. The sole of the pointe shoe is immoveable, or too hard?

Bend the shoe carefully. To do this you may need the help of a stronger pair of hands. With very hard shoes you can also use the crushing-in-the-door method. In this case, however, when bending the shoe, concentrate your efforts more on the sole. (see item 5, Tip 2).

Or else loosen half the insole from the rest of the shoe.

This makes the shoe more flexible, and the sole fits better to your foot (see item 14, from Tip 2 on).

14. The balance when on pointe is not ideal, you fall off pointe very quickly and can't stay up securely, the shoe changes shape?

● Check the platform and alter it if necessary with the pointe-darning technique (see item 2 and 3), this time darning the edge between the sole and the platform. If you now find that you can't get up on pointe, or that your balance is now too far forward, you must darn the opposite edge several times.

● Using a solid pair of scissors, pare down the various layers of the inner sole in steps, first loosening half of the inner sole from the outer sole.

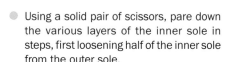

While doing this, bear in mind the varying thicknesses of the soles. After each stage of the operation, try the shoe out again.

If necessary, carefully remove the nails or staples in the outer and inner soles. With a screwdriver, lever them out a little by the head of the nail or staple.

Then pull them out completely with the screwdriver or a pair of pliers. Be careful! The best thing to do is to keep your hand over it as you work, so that the staples don't fly all over the place or hit you in the eye.

● Scoring wedge-shaped cuts into the outer sole is also an option (see item 8, Tip 2).

15. The instep needs to work better, to be shown to better advantage?

Take in the side pieces of the shoe. Look carefully at item 17.

Or else plane down the various soles, one step at a time (see item 14, Tip 2). You might want to shorten the entire insole by half. This is only to be recommended when you have completed your training.

16. The pointe shoe is too soft in the sole?

Strengthen the sole by inserting a rod of some flat, relatively inflexible material, like plastic or vulcanised fibre, about 1.5 cm. wide and 8 to 10 cm. long. You can easily get it from your pointe shoe maker or at a hardware shop. Wooden rods have shown themselves to be insufficiently flexible. They break easily and may hurt the foot.

You can also shorten them to the proper length as required and if necessary fasten them into the sole with strong glue.

The pointe shoe manufacturer Sansha supplies special rods made of plastic for this purpose.

Or pour in a special glue for pointe shoes, for example "Pointe Hardener" or shellac. Rock the shoe back and forth, so that the glue is evenly distributed, then allow to dry overnight. Make sure there's enough fresh air! You can also do this job with a brush, but you'll have to clean it very carefully afterwards.

The quarter – the heel section

17. The material is too high at the sides and especially on pointe it wrinkles or bulges. The instep of the foot needs better freedom to work, or the pointe shoe should sit better on the foot.

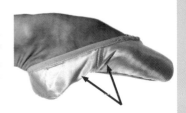

In this picture you can easily recognise the creation of unsightly wrinkles.

Cross-stitch sewing technique:

Sew the excess material on the inner side of the shoe together, using a cross-stitch. You can also use this on the outside if necessary. Start on the inner side of the shoe, behind the block. Fasten the thread at the beginning and end of the seam, again without a knot.

Stick the needle in diagonally on one side, and a little further along on the opposite side. As you work, pull, so that the stitch remains tight. This way the material will be preserved and at the same time held in place.

On the way up and down the seam, pull less and less cloth into the new seam near the ends, so that it can eventually be allowed to reach an end and run out.

On the way back, stitch diagonally across the seam again, forming a cross shape with the thread.

Finally, lead the yarn into the seam and make it "disappear".

To enhance the instep even further, you can also modify the insole (see from item 14, Tip 2 and onwards).

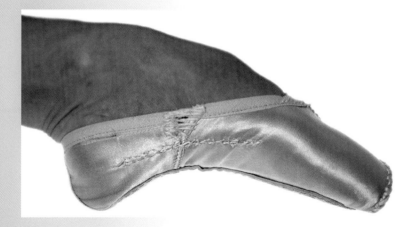

"Dance is above all the expression of joy, of light and not of darkness. Of course melancholy as with every other spiritual condition is sometimes used as the theme for a dance. However, it is born of joy, not of melancholy, and joy is what its continuous development produces."

Mikhail Fokine in discussion with Martha Graham

18. The pointe shoe is a little too small? There's too much pressure at the edges or in the heel area?

- Moisten the shoe from inside, and a little from the outside with some water, then put it on your bare foot so that it can stretch. If the material still doesn't give enough, try the following option:

- Separate or cut into the middle of the back seam about 1.5 to 2 centimetres. Then darn the cut as shown in the picture.

- Cut into the inner and outer sides, possibly even into the vamp (see item 6).

- If necessary, darn the cuts or insert a piece of elastic.

19. The shoe is too big?

Overlap the material on the inner side of the shoe.

Fasten the new seam, using the sewing technique mentioned under item 17.

TIP: Sometimes, when you pull the draw-string tight, it may tend to cut into your heel. If this happens, loosen it again, tighten it up just enough so that it fits comfortably on the heel, then sew it fast through the drawstring casing on both sides of the shoe. Afterwards you can pull it as tight as you want from the front.

Or else cut into or unpick the waist seam.

Overlap the excess material.

Darn the piece of material, using the cross-stitch technique (see item 17).

20. The foot doesn't have enough purchase in the heel or the side areas, the material is too short?

● Unpick only the inner seam of the drawstring casing at the heel. Simply turn up the material you have released, which can serve as an extension to the height of the heel.

● With some models, this can't be done, because the drawstring casing is graduated from the inside out. If this is the case, try the following: release the drawstring casing completely from the heel.

Sew up the underside of the drawstring casing again, using cross-stitching (see item 17).

● Or else darn the edge of the heel or the sides as well, in a pyramid shape, using the blanket-stitch technique.

Darn back and forth along the edge until you reach the desired height. Used the same technique as for the point (see item 2).

● Of course you can also sew on elastics (see items 36 to 38).

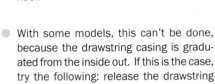

21. The heel is too big, the material is too high, causing the foot to lose its grip or sink into the shoe?

Take in the material of the inner and/or the outer sides, using the cross-stitch technique (item 17). Start at the heel, and finish halfway along, at or near the waist seam.

If necessary you can sew the seam in a half-moon shape, starting from the outer sole, sewing around the heel then back to the outer sole again. You can also start the seam at the side, as shown in the picture, then carry on as far as the heel.

Try this option: Undo the drawstring casing completely from the heel.

Then sew it on again, a little lower down.

Afterwards, simply cut away the excess material from the heel section.

Pointe shoe ribbons

There are many different types of pointe shoe ribbons, and several ways of fastening them to the shoes. Traditionally, the ribbons are sewn to the sides of the shoes, them tied over the foot. One can also pull a long ribbon through a slit in the side of the shoe. The picture above shows the version that I prefer. In this picture you can also see which modifications I have made to my shoes. Instead of tying the ribbons together, there is also an excellent alternative, which is to fasten them with Velcro. This method is especially good if your feet tend to change size while you are dancing. Recently manufacturers have now even begun to produce ribbons with short, built-in elastic inserts.

22. Which ribbons are used for sewing on or pulling through?

There are ribbons of different materials and varying widths. Some ribbons stretch slightly, others are less accommodating. As these ribbons are very expensive, I suggest that after using them, you remove them from the old shoes, so that you can re-use them on the next pair. Pointe shoe ribbons are generally pretty sturdy, and if you look after them they can last for a long time. You can of course use normal satin hair ribbon. Try it out!

You need to be aware, however, that all ribbons stretch and become longer because of sweat and body heat. When they dry, they shrink again. You will therefore have to try several different lengths to find the right dimensions for your own requirements.

Ribbons – sewing technique

23. Where is the right place to attach the ribbons?

- Fold the back seam forwards towards the point. The place where the edge of the material folds over is your starting point for attaching the ribbons.

The exact position of this point may vary somewhat, if for example you have a very high instep. Keep trying it out, till you find the spot that suits you.

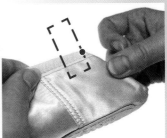

24. Where and how should the ribbons be sewn on?

- Sew the ribbons to the inside of the pointe shoe.

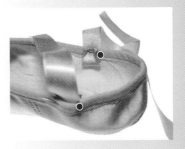

Fold the outer end of the ribbon over twice. This gives more strength, and helps to prevent fraying or unravelling.

Then sew the ribbons on at the point you have chosen, stitching in a square form-ation. For extra security you can also sew along the diagonals of the square.

TIP: Make sure that you sew the ribbons only onto the inner lining of the shoe, so that the stitches aren't visible from outside.

You can sew the inner ribbon on so that it slants slightly forwards, which will prevent wrinkling of the ribbon when you are in plié or when standing normally.

This is the last possible moment to decide which shoe is going to be left and which is right!

TIP: Be sure when attaching the ribbons that you don't sew through the drawstring.

25. How long should the ribbons be?

To find out exactly how long the ribbons need to be for each pair of pointe shoes, you can start off with two ribbons cut to at least 55 cm. If you want to work with just one ribbon, using the pull-through technique, then it's safest to start off with a total length of 120 cm. (see item 31).

Tack the ribbons to the shoe, lead them round your ankle and tie the knots. Now cut off the leftover material that hangs out of the knot, leaving a small margin.

When you undo the ribbons again, you will see that one ribbon is now longer than the other.

You will need to sew the longer ribbon to the inner side of the shoe, as it has further to go before reaching the place where the knot will be tied. You can now use both these ribbons as a pattern for cutting other pairs in the future.

Tying technique

26. How are pointe shoe ribbons tied around the foot?

There are many variations. I will show you two of the commonest methods. What's important in both methods is that you should always tie your ribbons when your ankle is bent (in plié) or flexed, otherwise they will be too tight and strangle your foot!

The first method requires you to cross the ribbons in front of your foot so that the outer ribbon (the blue ribbon in the photographs) is underneath, and the inner one on top. This is more flattering to your instep.

Now lead the ribbons around the anklebone, crossing them both, once behind and once in front of the ankle.

TIP: It looks better if you don't cross them exactly in front the second time, but slightly towards the inner side of the foot.

Now hold the outer ribbon fast and tie the inner one once more around the bone as far as the inner side of the foot.

TIP: If you pull the inner band a little tighter than the outer one, you will be able to get the shoe to "turn out" better on your foot.

Then tie the ribbons together as explained under item 27.

VARIATION 2

As in the first method, cross the ribbons over each other in front of the foot, first grasping the outer ribbon (the blue ribbon shown in the pictures) and leading it over the foot. The advantage of this second method is that the ribbons only cross once behind the ankle, so that they present a unified appearance from the front.

Now take the inner ribbon and lead it directly around your foot to the place where the knot will be tied. This ensures the "turn-out" of the shoe, and the inner ribbon looks better lying on top.

Hold the inner ribbon fast, and lead the outer ribbon (blue) around the foot.

Then you can knot the ribbons together (see item 27).

27. Where is the right place to tie the ribbons together?

Tie the ribbons together on the inner side of your ankle, between the bone and the Achilles tendon, where you will find a small anatomical hollow place which allows the knot to "disappear" completely.

A double (reef) knot works best. It holds extremely well, but it can also be undone easily. It needs a little practice.

28. How do you make the ends of the ribbons "invisible"?

● You can tuck the knots and the loose ends under the ribbon, either from above or from below.

● The surest way is to wind the ends around all the layers of ribbon and over the knot.

Then simply tuck the leftover ends in underneath.

29. The ends of ribbon come loose when you tuck them in?

● Put a sticking-plaster over or around them.

● Moisten the ends with water, or spread resin on them.

● The ends of ribbon are sometimes sewn onto the mound of material around the knot, or even to the dancer's tights.

TIP: As an alternative to knotting, I would recommend fastening the ribbons with Velcro (see item 34).

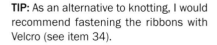

Irritating frayed ends

30. The ribbons or cut edges fray or run?

Cutting them off crooked instead of straight across can often appreciably hinder the tendency to fray.

A pinking shear can also do the job.

You can also darn the ends of the ribbons or the edges of the cuts.

Or else carefully seal the ribbons with a lighter. When you're doing this, just touch the protruding edges of the frayed area very lightly with the flame. Otherwise, the material may contract too tightly and form a hard edge, which will cause your tights to run and irritate your skin. You cannot use this technique with cotton ribbons.

Some dancers spray the cut edges with hairspray.

Pull-through technique

31. How do I use ribbons in the pull-through technique?

The advantage of this ribbon technique is that you only need one long ribbon per shoe. These ribbons can be made ready for use very quickly, and you can use them over and over again on successive pairs of shoes.

• Cut small slits, about 1.5 centimetres long, in the side of the shoe. In contrast to the sewing-on technique, this will need to be positioned a little closer to the heel, as the ribbon will slip forwards. Try it out until you find the place that suits you.

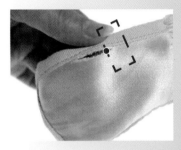

You can read about the length of the ribbons under item 25. Pull the ribbon through the slits on both sides of the shoe so that when you're wearing it, the ribbons will pass over your instep. Then carry on and tie them as normal.

My personal preference is for a combination of pull-through technique and Velcro fastenings (see item 35). This allows me to change shoes in a hurry if necessary, and also to adjust the tightness of the ribbons very quickly.

32. When I pull the ribbons through, they slide too far down my arch?

• Cut a small slit, about 1.5 centimetres, in the ribbon at the place where it crosses your foot. You can stop the cut edges from fraying by sealing them carefully with a lighter (see item 30).

33. What is the correct technique for tying pull-through ribbons with slits?

Once you have joined the ribbon to the side of the pointe shoe, pull the outer ribbon through the slit in the ribbon from above, then carry on to tie and knot the ribbons as explained under items 27 and 36. This technique gives the foot better tension.

"The true artist of the dance, or whatever one wants to call her, strives always for the higher beauty. Let us therefore become a world of artists, as we have already become a world of dancers! Thus wherever the ugly is replaced by the beautiful, in intangible matters as well as in visible things, we dance a little closer to happiness and completeness."

Anna Pavlova

Ribbons with Velcro fastenings

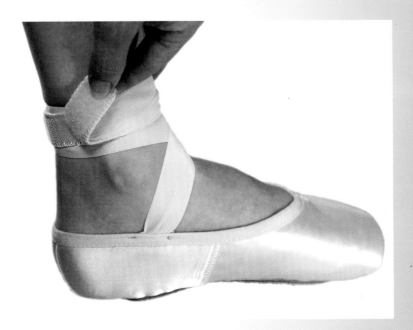

This method was "invented" at the Komische Oper in Berlin. In Tom Schilling's ballet *The Tales of Hoffmann*, the soloist who dances the role of Antonia has to do a really quick shoe change onstage in front of the audience. Immediately afterwards, having had just one chance to tie her shoes, she has to dance a difficult variation. It wasn't possible to re-tie the shoes onstage. It was an absolute horror. Even during the ensuing 32 fouettés, she had to be able to rely on these unaccustomed ribbons.

A way had to be found to cut down on the time needed to tie on the shoes. Someone in the costume department came up with the brilliant idea of using Velcro to fasten them. No sooner said than done.

When I took over this rôle, I too had to get used to these fastenings. However, even today, I use only this safest of fastening techniques. For quick changes, or when I'm nervous, it's simply the easiest way to undo and re-tie. And if the foot swells or shrinks, it's wonderfully quick and uncomplicated to make the necessary adjustment. However, before sewing it onto your ribbons, you ought to try out which sort of Velcro you need to use.

34. You need to be able to get your ribbons tied and untied quicker, and the fit adjusted rapidly?

Attach a strip of Velcro to the end of each ribbon; sew the soft part onto the inner surface of the outer ribbon, and the hard part onto the outside of the inner ribbon. This way you can prevent the hard surface of the Velcro from rasping against your skin or your tights.

Round off the corners of the Velcro strips beforehand. How much Velcro you will need is something you will have to find out by trial and error, although to be safe you need at least 6 centimetres.

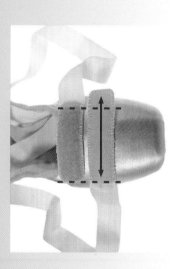

If your foot tends to swell or shrink while you are dancing, you will need to use longer, firm Velcro strips. This makes it easy to shorten or lengthen the ribbons quite quickly.

You can find out about the proper length for your ribbons under item 25.

35. How do you get ribbons with Velcro strips attached to them through the slits and fastened round the foot?

Pull the end with the soft Velcro carefully through the holes. Start from the inside of the shoe, so that this end will become your outer ribbon.

If necessary then pull it through the slit in the ribbon, and carry on to tie as already described.

When you're fastening the ribbons, the hard side of the Velcro should be the lower of the two surfaces. Now you merely need to press the end with the soft material down on top of it.

Now you can quickly and easily change or adjust the length of your pointe shoe ribbons.

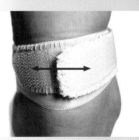

If you happen some time to find that you've sewn the Velcro onto the wrong side of the ribbon, you can also simply twist the ends of the ribbon.

With this combination of Velcro fastenings and the pull-through technique, it is possible to re-position the fastening to different places on your leg, as required. This is only possible to a limited extent if you're working through a slit in the ribbon itself (see item 33).

Elastics

36. Your foot is not held firmly enough inside the pointe shoe in the heel and ankle areas?

Sew a little loop of elastic in front of the back seam (at the Achilles tendon) onto the inside or the outside of the shoe. This elastic loop is there so that you can pull your pointe shoe ribbons through it. Use ordinary elastic.

However, this method can cause irritation to the Achilles tendon, so that quite often the following alternative is used:

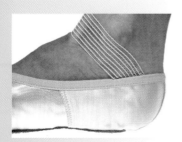

Fasten a loop of wide elastic from one side of the shoe to the other, passing under or behind the ankle-bone. For this you can use either ordinary or else somewhat wider elastic.

37. You are not allowed to wear ribbons with pointe shoes or flat shoes, or you need a better grip inside the shoe for your foot?

- Sew two wide, net-like elastics onto your shoes, just under the ankle-bone. Cross them over your instep, and fasten them to the other side of the shoe. The rear-most of the two inner elastics should lie on top of the crossover, as this gives the elastics a better line and shows off your foot to its best advantage.

- You can, however, also attach very firm elastics.

- In the case of soft shoes which already have elastic sewn on, you can join the ends together as shown in the picture. Pull the shoe on as usual, cross the loop of elastic over your instep, then pull it forward completely over the foot. The elastic now leads all the way round under the sole, and pulls the shoe firmly in to your foot.

38. The vamp is too low, you need more support for the instep?

- Attach a very broad elastic to the shoe so that it passes over the forward part of the instep (see item 6).

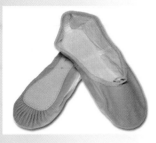

Soft shoes ("flatties")

39. What are soft shoes? What should I be using for class?

Soft shoes, or "flatties" are soft ballet slippers, used for class, rehearsal and performance. They are made of either leather or material, both kinds with single or split sole.

Soft shoes made of material are very popular both with beginners and with professionals, because they are simply much easier to dance and work with.

If you prefer more grip and resistance when executing the exercises, you will probably like a leather shoe with a single sole better.

Sometimes these shoes, too, have ribbons sewn onto them, to give the foot more resistance when working or to make the shoe look more like a pointe shoe.

Soft shoes are available in various colours. If you can't find the model you want, you can of course always order it in a dance-wear shop or over the Internet. You can also dye it yourself (see the chapter on "Dyeing").

Bear in mind that all models of soft shoe stretch when you work with them. For this reason, never buy soft shoes too large. If soft shoes of material do turn out to be too big, wash them in very hot water.

40. What are "cannibalised" pointe shoes?

"Cannibalised" shoes are old or new pointe shoes that have been modified to serve as soft shoes.

If, for example, you find that normal soft shoes are too soft for class, and your pointe shoes feel too hard and inflexible, then you should try out "cannibalised" pointe shoes. They help to ensure a good transition from using soft textile or leather shoes in class to using pointe shoes.

"Cannibalised" shoes do retain some parts of the original pointe shoe. There are several variations on the theme. In some methods, nothing is removed from the pointe shoe, it is merely made softer and more flexible. Other methods involve taking used or sometimes even new pointe shoes apart.

41. Why do people use "cannibalised" shoes?

The feet, ligaments, tendons and muscles have to work harder in them. More effort is required to overcome the resistance of the shoe and the ribbons. I personally prefer these "cannibalised" shoes for class. I usually remove only part of the insole, and I find this makes the transition to working on pointe easier.

42. How do you "cannibalise" a shoe?

Start with the insole. Either remove the sole completely, or simply trim off the layers one at a time, as though peeling an onion. Sometimes only half the sole is removed.

First, however, you'll need to prise up the tacks or nails from the inner and outer sole, and remove them. Then you'll have to get to work on the block (see chapter on "The Sole – Inner"). If this is impossible at first, dip the shoe into very hot water and knead it, so that the glue dissolves.

To get the reinforcement of the toe box out of the block, you will then need to cut round the material in the block.

Then turn the material of the block and the toe-box inside out. You can remove the excess material. The degree of difficulty in removing the toe-box will depend on the make and model of shoe.

Now turn the material of the vamp the right way round again, tidy them up a little if necessary, and your "cannibalised" shoes are ready.

They still look very much like normal pointe shoes. Now, however, they have the characteristics of soft textile shoes or "flatties".

If the insole is still prickly or rough on your foot, you can simply stick on a bandage as a replacement sole. You might have to sew it fast in a couple of places, to prevent it from peeling itself off.

Dyeing

It very often happens that costumes which have been specially designed and created for ballets or in dance pieces require shoes in colours that tone. In this case the job of dyeing pointe or soft shoes is often taken over by the theatre.

Sometimes, however, you have to do it yourself. Or perhaps you just want to dye your shoes, ribbons or tights of your own accord. Here are a couple of options:

43. How do I dye my pointe shoes, soft shoes and ribbons?

● If you're merely trying to get them to look a little less shiny, you can rub some resin into the surface. Use cotton wool or paper towels to rub with. If neither of these is to hand you can of course always use your finger. Although it'll be a bit sticky afterwards.

To change the colour of the material you can use water-soluble body make-up or non-fat cream make-up. You can also use skin-coloured powder. However powder makes the dance floor very slippery, so use it sparingly! Afterwards you should put some resin on the sole of the shoe, to prevent slipping.

If the shoe has to be a very strong colour such as white, black or red, I recommend using silk dye. It's easy to apply, and is only slightly shiny.

When you're using silk dye, bear in mind that the colour needs to be applied as thinly as possible, using a light sponge, so that the material doesn't shrink and bunch together. Theatre shoemakers even spray the colour on, so as to avoid this risk.

The difference between using body make-up or using silk dye is that body make-up leaves a powdery film of colour on the pointe shoe, which you can actually wipe off by carefully rubbing with a paper or textile handkerchief. Silk dye, in contrast, doesn't rub off once it has dried.

Generally speaking, you shouldn't dye pointe shoes and soft shoes too wet, as the material will shrink appreciably in drying. If despite your efforts the shoe has still become a little too small, it will open out again the next time it is moistened. I recommend therefore that you put the shoes on at once, as soon as they have been dyed or moistened, to avoid shrinkage. You can use a shoe horn to help you get them on.

If you want your ribbons, tights and so on to have a beige tone, you can dye them with black tea, or with water that has been used for boiling onion peels.

If you want to dye white objects or material pink, simply use rose-hip or hibiscus tea.

Put several bags of the chosen variety of tea into boiling water. To retain the strong colour of the water, leave the bag in it for a few minutes longer.

When you've taken them out, gently put in the material you want to dye, making sure that it has already been moistened. When dyeing, make sure that all the cloth is under the surface of the water, otherwise your colour will be patchy and spotty.

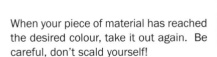

When your piece of material has reached the desired colour, take it out again. Be careful, don't scald yourself!

Then rinse it thoroughly in tepid water.

Cleaning

44. How do I clean shoes and ribbons?

You can clean pointe shoes and soft shoes by wiping them off with a damp cloth and some washing-up liquid (or cleaning solvent). In the latter case, make sure there is enough ventilation.

You can cover small stains with a little resin or some water-soluble make-up. If there is only powder available, use it very sparingly and not too thickly on the sole, otherwise there is a danger of slipping.

Beside this it is also entirely possible to wash soft shoes, tights and even cannibalised pointe shoes (with a cloth outer covering, and without insole) in the washing machine or by hand.

With both types of soft shoe, though, shortly before they're completely dry, you should put them on, so that they don't shrink. If, even so, they have become smaller, you can moisten them lightly with water and immediately put them on, as described in the section on Dyeing. Generally this will cause them to stretch a little.

After washing, or dyeing your pointe shoe ribbons with tea, pull them through a dry towel. This way they won't shrink while drying, and you won't have to iron them.

Durability

45. The "life-span" of pointe shoes and soft shoes

Try always to keep your pointe shoes and soft shoes well ventilated, so that they can dry out after the rehearsal. While you're dancing, a lot of sweat will run into your pointe shoe, easily as much as half a litre in an hour. For this reason, never shut your pointe shoes up in a plastic bag, because it allows no way out for the leftover moisture. Because of this, your shoes will very quickly "give up the ghost", sooner than necessary.

Pointe shoes harden up again when the damp is removed from them. It's quicker if you put them on or under a radiator, depending on how quickly you need to dry them. You can also leave them in the oven at 50°C overnight to harden off, or stuff them with newspaper and paper towels. But in the latter instance, you should change the paper often.

If you want to extend the hardness and firmness of your shoes over a longer period, you can soak them in special pointe shoe glue or insert a special rod to strengthen the insole (see the chapters on "The Pointe", "The Block", and "The Sole – inner").

If wear and tear has caused your shoes to develop holes, you can simply darn them, just as you would darn a sock. However, while you're doing this, keep trying them on to make sure they haven't now become too small. But you can also cover half of the outer sole of the soft shoe by applying a sticking-plaster. To stop it from coming loose or peeling off while you work, you will have to stitch down the edges.

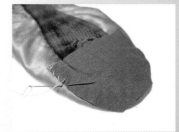

A ballerina's tricks

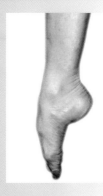  

In the photos you can see the foot of a successful Principal Dancer. In spite of her very well-trained arch, she still carries out modifications to the original shoe, so as to be able to work better with it.

The first picture shows the line of her foot, once with no shoe, then comparing an unmodified shoe with a pointe shoe that has been especially adapted to her needs. This is not about making the shoe look more beautiful. What is much more important is that the shoe after it has been tuned supports the foot as well as possible, and that the foot is shown to its best advantage, even when seen from a distance.

Her working procedures, step by step

She has darned around the edge of the platform, to achieve the largest possible surface on which to stand or turn and to reduce the chances of slipping on the stage floor.

She has kneaded the block to make it softer, but otherwise she has made no changes, as the vamp is already the perfect height for her metatarsus and supports her instep satisfactorily.

She has also soaked the insole with pointe shoe glue to make it harder, and to improve support and durability.

She has sewn elastics to the sides, so that the shoe lies snugly against her foot and the sole of the shoe is in better contact with the sole of her foot. This way, the pointe shoe fits the foot better and more firmly. Her foot doesn't have to hold onto the shoe, it can look after its own priorities.

She has sewn the ribbons on and tied them normally. She didn't know about the pull-through technique.

"Dance is Life"

PRECAUTIONS

BETTER SAFE THAN SORRY!

In this part of the book you will encounter some exercises and practices that can help to strengthen your feet and keep them healthy. The choice of exercises was arrived at after, among other things, collaboration with my long-term physiotherapist, Sabine Müller, who has been with me through thick and thin during my dancing career at the Komische Oper Berlin, and even today still stands by me always, with sound advice and help.

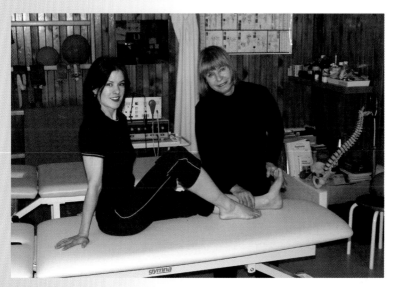

How does it go? An ounce of prevention is worth a pound of cure. The modifications to your pointe shoes that I have offered in this book are no guarantee that your foot will always remain secure and undamaged. It can grow as well, or change its constitution. Not all of the muscles in your foot are really working when you're on pointe, as they are a bit cramped inside the shoe, and are thus held in a particular position. Even so, you need them to be fit in order to dance.

So I want to advise you, not only on the basis of my own experience, to strengthen your feet with small but extremely effective therapeutic exercises, as well as doing your regular work in pointe shoes. These exercises help to strengthen the small muscles as well, and the tendons and ligaments of your foot. They also ensure that your toes, ankles, calf muscles and knees will become stronger and more secure. You will even notice their strengthening effect in your pelvis and your back.

The particular thing about these exercises is that the strengthened muscular apparatus also affects your co-ordination. If you do these exercises regularly, you will soon be able to make better use of the space in which you dance, and will find out quicker how to master it. Dancing, with or without pointe shoes, will seem appreciably easier.

A little fitness primer

This ABC of exercises ought to contribute to the strengthening of your toes, your longitudinal and transverse arches, your ankle joint and your calves. The exercises help you to avoid injury or strain to feet and ankles. Correct execution and the controlled use of your strength are always very important. I have intentionally used pictures of a girl whose feet and muscles still need to be developed for dance.

"The Ball"

You will need a rubber ball, as big as a ping-pong ball. Aim at your "victim" with your toes, grasp it in your toes and pick it up.

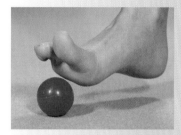

Let it go, then go on the "attack" again. Repeat the exercise several times.

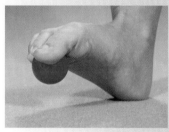

You can also work very well with a large foam ball, kneading it against the floor with your toes or squeezing it together in the air by pressing firmly inwards on it with the soles of your feet.

You can also try to pick up the foam ball with your toes.

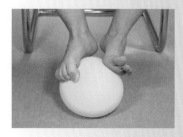

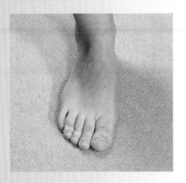

"The Flippers"

This exercise helps the relaxation and strengthening of your toe muscles and ligaments by loosening and stretching. It also helps to reduce pain in the ball of the foot. As your foot cannot work in its natural position when it Is confined inside a pointe shoe, I recommend that you do this little exercise as often as you can.

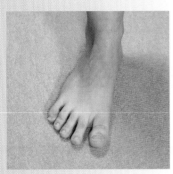

Spread your toes as if you were wearing flippers, and hold this position for a while. Then relax the foot.

"The Cinderella"

This exercise acts to strengthen your entire foot (toes, metatarsus and ankle joint).

To do it, take two bowls or similar containers. One of them should contain peas or beans or anything small that you can pick up with your toes. The other bowl is empty. Now, using only your toes, dig into the contents of the first bowl like a mechanical digger and get a grip on the contents.

Then drop your catch into the other bowl. Continue the exercise, alternating feet regularly, until the first bowl is empty. If you still feel like it, you can now repeat the exercise until the second bowl is empty. If there are no suitable bowls to hand, you can also use the floor (claw them up – hold – drop).

You can tear up a paper towel with your toes. Put the paper down on a smooth surface, stand on it and scrunch it up in your toes. Now move your feet apart, keeping the heels on the floor. You can also combine this exercise with the previous one by picking up the shreds of paper in your toes and carrying them to the waste-paper basket. You can also do this exercise in a sitting position. (scrunch up – tear up – drop)

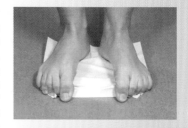

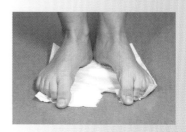

"The sand- or mattress-runner"

This exercise has a strengthening effect on your toes and the muscles of your lower leg.

You need a thick, soft mattress, one that your foot can really sink into while you are working.

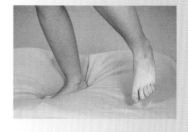

Imagine to yourself that the mattress is full of grapes, and that you have been engaged as a grape-treader. While you're doing this exercise, your muscles will tire very quickly. However this exercise has a really important effect on your training, as your foot has to work very efficiently to deal with all the different angles of tread (front, back, side and so on) and adjust to the resulting transfer of weight.

On the other hand if you should happen to find yourself near a beach, you can do the same exercise as on the mattress, only this time on sand. If at the same time you walk or run in the water, there is also a healthy tonic effect, because the cold water also improves your circulation.

You can also "knead" the sand with your toes, like a baker kneading bread. You can also execute this sand exercise in a sandbox, in either a standing or a sitting position.

"The Caterpillar Walk"

This has a strengthening effect on the structure of the foot, the calf and the thigh as well as on the pelvis and the back. It looks a little like the crawling gait of the caterpillar. The best way to do this exercise is on a carpet-like surface. Linoleum would be too cold for the soles of the feet.

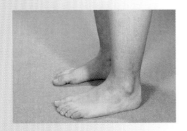

To get into the start position, stand bare-foot on the carpet. The legs are slightly apart, in a line with your pelvis. The knees are slightly bent, and pointing forwards, as are your toes.

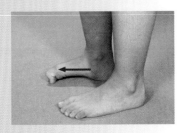

Now curl up the toes of the right foot, so that your heel moves forward towards the toes. Make sure that you don't tip the foot onto the outer edge, as shown in the picture! Carry on this sequence, alternating right foot, then left foot and so on.

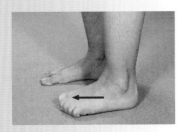

When you change feet, make a conscious decision to put the arch of the other foot down to the floor. What is important here is to keep the heel on the floor at all times.

Now you can also do it "in reverse": Don't set off immediately in search of the wide open spaces, just simply reverse the sequence. To do this, start by curling up your toes, although this time don't pull the heel towards them. Only when you stretch the toes does the heel slide backwards, so that finally your foot is flat on the floor again. This sequence, too, is done with alternating feet: right, left and so on.

It makes sense to set yourself a distance to cover, e.g. two times 1 meter, or four times 50 centimetres. You decide when you need a break. Don't make it too long, otherwise the effect of the training will be diminished. Your muscles will soon give you the right "tempo".

"The strong hand"

This exercise has a strengthening effect on the muscles of your foot, calf and shin. You don't need any machines, only your hands, which will be your opponents during the execution of the exercise. They provide the resistance necessary to the strengthening of the muscles. Make sure that during the exercise, your neck muscles stay as relaxed as possible! While you're doing this exercise, sit comfortably on a warm floor.

Hold onto your toes with your hands. Then wrap your fingers around your toes and try to press them downwards against resistance. Hold this position for a moment. Repeat the exercise several times from the beginning.

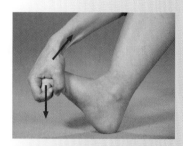

You can also combine this exercise with another one. To do so, put your hand over the still curled-up toes and then push with outstretched toes against your hand.

You can reinforce the effect of the first exercise by moving your whole foot against the resistance of your hand, stretching the foot towards the floor.

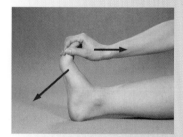

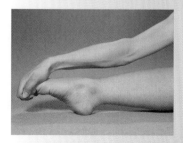

"The Wall"

In the next exercise, your hands form a barrier to the left and right of your flexed or stretched foot.

Now flex your foot. Push one hand against the inner side of the foot, and the other against the outer side, starting at the toes and covering the foot as far as the heel.

The foot always resists the pressure. Now work backwards from the end position to the starting point. You can also try to push your hand away with your foot. You decide how often you want to repeat the exercise.

These exercises where your hand wraps around the toes or acts as a barrier are also variable. You can provide resistance at specific points only, or work with one toe at a time, to concentrate on your own special "problem zones".

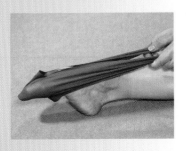

You can also do the exercises with the help of special rubber bands which you can buy in sporting goods shops.

Starting position – curl up – press against resistance – hold the position – relax

"The short foot"

An exercise which looks like nothing at all, but produces a phenomenal effect. Start in a sitting position, so that you can keep an eye on your feet. Later on you can do this exercise standing up.

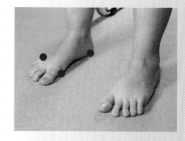

• Start off barefoot, with the feet a pelvis width apart, then spread your toes as far as possible, as in the "Flipper" exercise. Feel the contact with the floor. Above all, make sure all three pressure points are in constant contact with the floor, otherwise the exercise won't have the desired effect. The three points are found on the ball of the foot, just behind the big toe, just behind the little toe and at the heel.

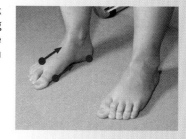

Now pull the front part of your foot back towards the heel, without, however, losing floor contact with the three pressure points. You will see that by doing this, you cause your foot to "shorten".

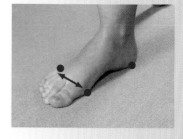

Then widen both feet as far as you can outwards, as though you were trying to flatten out the floor. This won't be so easy at first. You will soon feel the tension in your feet and ankles. After a couple of seconds, you can relax, then start again after a short rest.

Finish off the exercise by lightly shaking your feet, to help them to relax quicker. However, if you have lost floor contact with one of the three pressure points mentioned above, you should do the whole exercise again from the beginning. Don't despair! In the beginning, it can easily happen.

"The Stairs"

You can use this exercise to strengthen your ankles and stretch your calf muscles. It's very good for building up strength in the legs after a holiday or an injury.

Find a staircase which has a banister for you to hold onto. Any other large step upwards will also do just as well for this exercise. Now stand with your feet on the edge of the step. Only the balls of your feet should be touching the step. The toes point forwards, and your heels are suspended in the air.

Now carefully transfer your weight onto the heels. You'll feel a pulling sensation in your calf muscles. This causes your calf muscles, tendons and ligaments to be stretched. Possible cramps, tensions or muscle pains will immediately announce their presence. You should hold the position for a little (about 10 seconds) and breathe while you are in the stretched position. Then return to the starting position.

You can now repeat the entire sequence. This time, however, the exercise ends not in the starting position but on half-pointe (in the relevé position). This time your calf muscles are tensed.

Repeat the exercise a couple of times, returning each time to the starting position, until your muscles are tired. Then stretch your calf muscles again, as at the beginning of the exercise. Depending on how they feel, you can give the calves or feet a short rest by shaking them a little.

For a change you can do this exercise on an aerobics step (for condition), or else on one leg only. As your entire weight is going to be on this leg, you'll feel an increased training effect.

Be careful in all exercises to listen to the signals given by your body, and to go only to the limits of the load your feet can carry, and not beyond it!

"The Russian dance" – variation 1

You should do this exercise on the right and left sides.

Stand on a warm surface (either with socks on or in bare feet). Your feet are parallel, slightly apart at hip-width. Knees are slightly bent, and facing forwards.

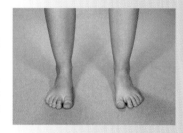

Now start by transferring the weight slightly onto the balls of the feet. To move to your right, turn both heels (from the hips) to the right. Your upper body stays unchanged facing the original direction. You can use your arms to balance against the movement.

Describe a half-circle with your heels, put them down on the floor and transfer the weight onto them. Now lift the front part of your feet off the floor and bring them too in a half-circle to your right, put them down and transfer your weight onto them.

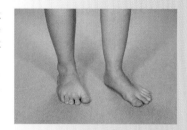

Keep going until you feel a pulling sensation in the muscles of your feet, calves and shins. In this exercise, that's always a good sign that the muscles are working.

After a short rest you can do this exercise in the opposite direction. If you do it on one leg, you are also training your balance.

Stand – weight onto front of foot – lift heels – make a half-circle – lower heels – weight onto heels – lift front of foot – draw half-circle – lower front of foot – weight onto front of foot etc.

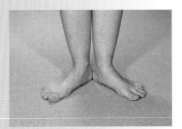

"The Russian dance" – variation 2

For this variation, start with a slightly open position of the feet, heels touching and toes pointing diagonally outwards. Your knees are as always slightly bent. This is your starting position.

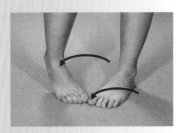

Here too, you move both feet at the same time. Only now one foot will be turning in and the other foot will be turning out.

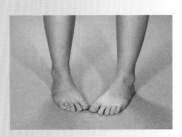

The difference between this and the previous exercise is that your weight will be on the ball of one foot and the heel of the other, so that you can go on.

Then you can cross your arms, maybe you've got some atmospheric music playing, and immediately your "Russian dance" is perfect!

3-minute programme for the circulation of the foot

- Lie down and raise your legs to 90°. Rotate the feet for 30 seconds, once to the right and once to the left to loosen and relax the ankles. In every exercise when you lie on the floor, make sure you're not arching your back!

- Alternate flexing and stretching the feet for a minute (to strengthen the muscles). You can support your legs in this exercise by leaning them against a wall.

- Then walk about barefoot on your heels for one minute. This has the effect of strengthening the shin muscles. After that, walk on the balls of the feet. Alternate the position of the feet every 15 seconds.

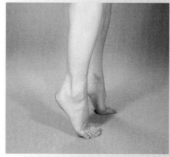

Warm-up and relaxation techniques

Before taking on heavy work, you should prepare your body and your mind by getting them ready for the coming hours with a few light exercises. In order to avoid injury, you need to warm up from the inside out, in other words through physical activity. Start with light exercises and combinations to lubricate the joints, loosen and stretch tendons and ligaments, and warm up your muscles. During the warm-up, substances are released which deliver the necessary energy for your muscles.

To keep your body warm on the outside, it's not enough just to wrap it up well. Good training saves you the otherwise inevitable "running-in" phase, in order to get going for a rehearsal or a performance. Later on you will almost certainly set up your own programme for warming up before hard physical work and cooling down afterwards.

"Well-being programme" that gets the body ready to go:

Walk and jog in a circle (forwards, backwards and sideways) to activate your circulation.

Bicycle, while lying on your back (forwards and backwards).

Roll back and forth on the floor. Let your extremities flop, them stretch them.

Circle the arms, legs and feet, to loosen the joints and lubricate them.

Only stretch your muscles when they are thoroughly warmed up! When stretching always breathe deep in your muscles (when breathing out).

 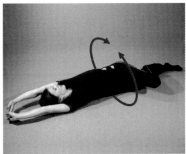

Breathing

You should devote a lot of attention to your breathing. Through intense muscular contraction, the body and the organs are well supplied with blood during breathing. If you hold your breath too long during an exercise, the supply of oxygen to the muscles is hindered or curtailed. They get tired very quickly, and lose their elasticity. Soon you will feel exhausted, hanging like washing on the line. While dancing I have actually managed, by not breathing regularly, to tire myself out completely after a preparation (which is the name we give to the setting up of a step, before its actual execution). My pulse was racing, even before I began to dance. Incorrect breathing technique coupled with pre-performance nerves can rob you of all your strength!

It's also much easier to deal with stage-fright if you breathe with a conscious, regular rhythm. Dancing become easier and much more enjoyable.

Relaxation

Simply kneel down on the floor on top of some warm surface. Sit down on your heels and lay your upper body over your legs (curl up like a hedgehog). Your head rests on the floor, and your arms are stretched out in front of you or beside you.

Concentrate on the sensation in your stomach and back, and take note of your breathing, so that you feel, for example, how each new intake of breath fills the muscles in your back and your abdomen. Feel how they stretch and grow, as though an angel's wings were opening and closing. When you breathe out, the muscles relax better, and tensions are more easily released.

The following exercise is one that I find very comfortable for my back, but above all for my head.

To do the exercise, lay your hands beside your head as in the relaxation exercise above. Then take a little of your weight on your hands. Now "roll" carefully back and forth on your head. Always use your arms to control the placement of your weight. This stretches the neck muscles and the gentle massage invigorates the head.

For the next exercise, lie on your back, then take hold of your feet and swing them up over your head, keeping the knees slightly bent.

In this position you can now rock gently on your back, from the spinal column all the way up to your neck, thereby stretching and massaging your muscles.

Foot hygiene

Blisters

If you find that your are getting blisters and soft corns on your feet, you need to know that these are caused mostly by the shoe rubbing on your still very sensitive skin, as a result of dampness which arises in the shoe in the course of your work. If inflammation occurs, blisters and soft corns can become a real scourge. This can happen very easily, and it doesn't necessarily indicate bad hygiene. However, you can still do a lot to prevent this disagreeable accompaniment to your dancing.

● You can prepare your feet for the load they are going to have to take by working them over and scrubbing them with an abrasive sponge, for example, while on holiday. This will toughen them up. Many people also massage propolis salve into the toes, to prevent the formation of blisters.

● If necessary, you can just bandage the blisters, or make use of other pain relief methods (see item 7). Some people line their block with lambswool, cotton wool, toilet paper or soft cleaning cloths. Dancewear shops also stock special liners of varying materials for use inside the block. To prevent blisters you can also tape or bandage your toes with zinc oxide tape or with normal sticking plaster.

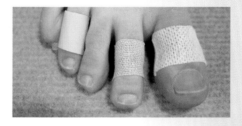

● You can also wind strips of paper towel between your toes. These absorb sweat during your work, thereby preventing the development of athlete's foot or soft corns. You need to change the paper towels several times a day, however, or else you will produce the opposite effect.

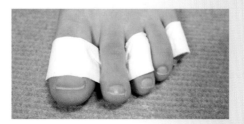

Soft Corns

When dealing with soft corns you should try to release the pressure on the affected area. You can do this by, for example, using a piece of foam rubber or a special foam bandage with a hole in it. Use disinfectant powder as well, to keep the area dry and get rid of any infection there may be. There are also ointments and special varnishes for treating calluses and soft corns, and you can buy these at the chemist's. If none of these helps, than it would be best to ask for medical advice.

Many experienced teachers advise dancers who are just beginning on pointe to manage without any padding around the metatarsus. This way the foot is better able to feel the shoe and get to know it. I always work without any padding in my shoes.

If you have only just started working on pointe, your skin will gradually become accustomed to the demands made on it. It will become firmer and harder. Usually calluses will develop at the places that start as pressure points, and these will act as a natural protection against blisters.

Toenails

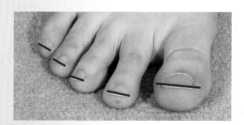

Toenails which are too long get very crushed and bent when working on pointe. If you're not careful, they can easily become ingrown, giving rise to infection in the bed of the nail.

This is why ideally you should work on your toenails after your bath, or after class. But be careful when you're cutting them! The nails will be very soft, so they can be cut very quickly and easily. I would advise you, however, not to shorten them too far, or you will find pointe work painful.

By the way, you should cut your nails straight across, not like the foot of the girl in the photo. This will distribute the load evenly across the nail and prevent ingrown toenails.

Practice gear

Your practice gear should be comfortable and not too tight, so as not to impede your freedom of movement. Pullovers, pants and overalls of cotton or fleece are suitable for wearing over your tights. They keep the muscles and joints warm, and are comfortable next to the skin. These materials are especially suited for keeping the body warm before or after class, in between rehearsals or backstage.

Dancers also like to wear outer clothing of anorak material. However, these don't let enough air through. After effort, the muscles certainly stay warm, but they tire quicker. Also, the layer beneath your outer clothing gets very damp. This can soon cause you to catch cold.

As far as I am concerned, outer clothes of fleece over my tights have proven very valuable, especially in open air performances and in various types of weather conditions. Fleece keeps the body warm, allows moisture to pass through and disperse, and still keeps draughts out. Also thick socks, leg-warmers, slippers of soft material, fleece or leather into which I can shuffle my pointe shoes – all of these belong to my classic keep-warm materials.

And what if you get injured?

Injuries are usually preceded by minor physical problems which we either discover too late or else simply ignore for the sake of dancing. Because we dancers learn early to see pain not exclusively as an enemy (as with aching muscles, for example), we often work right up to or past our natural pain threshold. We often find it very difficult to know exactly which is the right moment to allow our body a little rest. Maybe there's a performance which you simply must dance, because it is your absolute dream rôle, or else you are considered to be irreplaceable. Oh just this one rôle! This performance! These few small pains! Stopping sooner would certainly have cost you less recovery time.

Even so! The injuries which one can now and again inflict on oneself in the course of one's dancing career should never be seen as negative experiences. I think of it as a momentary pause. These inconveniences give me the opportunity to get to know the requirements of my body, and to understand my physical and mental limits. This doesn't mean, however, that these limits must unconditionally be accepted.

So don't let yourself become discouraged, because these enforced pauses help you to think again about your habits and your dream of dancing.

"If you wish to become a dancer, you must learn not to fear pain. You must teach your body to obey you. You must learn to control your body, every muscle, every nerve, every cell. The body does not control the dancer, but instead teaches her how to be the ruler of her own body... We teach our bodies not to question our instructions."

A Ballet-Master to Anna Pavlova

Granny's special recipes

For more serious disorders, please always consult a doctor! However, you can often deal perfectly well with the smaller aches and pains by yourself.

Blisters: Lay an alcohol-soaked cloth over the place. This soothes the pain and draws out the moisture. You can also put raw egg onto the inner skin of the afflicted spot. When it is dry, put a plaster over it to keep it in place. This second skin is said to take away the pain caused by touch, and to promote quicker healing. Sometimes raw meat is used as blister protection inside the block.

Soft corns: It is supposed to be helpful to lay a slice of fresh garlic on the place every morning and evening. Rubbing pork fat or soft soap into endangered areas is also considered helpful as a preventive measure.

Cold feet: Soak your socks in brine, which you make with normal salt and water. Put the socks on and put on another, dry pair on top of them. This promotes circulation in the foot and is also good for the skin. When your feet are warm again, simply take the socks off again and wash your feet.

Calf-muscle pains, problems with the Achilles tendon: As well as stretching and massage (with a tennis ball or a golf ball for example) a hot, damp compress is also helpful. To make one, wrap a very hot, damp towel around your calf, then a dry towel over it. This ensures improved circulation and relaxes the muscles.

Wounds and cuts: Lay the fine membrane from between layers of onion on the wound; this has an antiseptic effect. Hold it in place with a light, porous dressing. Wounds that are slow in healing can be treated by brushing on some honey; this is a time-honoured remedy. For small burns, apply a little butter and a thin slice of potato. Burn blisters should not be punctured!

Inflammation or stub injuries: Make a cabbage compress (either white or green cabbage), by removing some of the outer leaves and flattening them, preferably with a rolling pin. This releases the juices and allows the healing parts of the plant to come fully into operation. Lay the leaves over the affected part and fasten them in place with a bandage. This particular compress must be changed several times until the inflammation has subsided. You can also make compresses out of cottage cheese to cool the injury. In the old days they even used to make compresses out of raw meat, because meat keeps the coolness for a very long time.

Muscle tension: Hot mashed potato in a cloth bag can also be used as a hot compress.

None of these foodstuffs are suitable for consumption after use!

"Wild Flower"

AND FINALLY

In a way, a pointe shoe is somehow almost like a partner for the dancer, her best friend, so to speak. It is her constant companion, onstage and backstage. It follows her faithfully home and is caressed and looked after by her, and sometimes scolded. There are times when she wants nothing to do with it. Mostly though, she can't stay away from it, for her sheer longing to rise up with it onto pointe again.

Well, I hope I've been able to help you with a couple of problems. As your training and your dancing life progress, new questions will arise. You will grow, your feet will change. Your demands on yourself and on your shoes will be different. Even then this book will still contain good advice for you.

I have enjoyed sharing my knowledge and experience with you, because in the end we share the same dream. May it come true for you too! I wish you stamina, the necessary patience, and a big slice of luck along your way.

Yours, Angela Reinhardt

Acknowledgements

Here I would like to say a special thank you once again to so many people who have helped me with their advice and their actions during the preparation of this book.

My thanks to Karin Schmidt-Feister for editorial help, to the physiotherapist Sabine Müller, to Jeremy Leslie Spinks for the translation into English, the pointe shoe makers Wolfgang Weigt and Kornelia Reisner, the chairman of the Deutsche Berufsverband für Tanzpädagogik, Ulrich Roehm, the Directress of the Staatliche Ballettschule Berlin, Hannelore Trageser, the editor of *ballett-tanz*, Hartmut Regitz, the foot models Sandy Delasalle (Principal Dancer) and Simone Edom, my son Christopher for the written work on the computer, and not least my husband, Mike-Martin Robacki for his collaboration on the text, his photographs, and the graphic design of the book.

Bibliography

Dancing Star – The Story of Anna Pavlova by Gladys Malvern – Julian Messner, New York 1942. *Die Welt des Tanzes in Selbstzeugnissen* by Lydia Wolgina and Ulrich Pietzsch – Henschel Verlag, Berlin 1980. *The Book of Ballet* by Fernando Reyna – Aimery Somogy, Paris. *Ballett A - Z* by Eberhardt Rebling – Henschel Verlag, Berlin 1980. *Ballerina – Women In Classical Ballet* by Mary Clarke and Clement Crisp, – vgs verlagsgesellschaft, Cologne 1988. *Knaurs Buch vom Tanz – Der Tanz durch die Jahrhunderte* (English title : *Dance Through The Centuries*) by Walter Sorell – Droemersche Verlagsgesellschaft Th. Knaur Nachf., Zürich 1969. *Mein Instrument der Körper* von Frauke Hofert – Sayla-Verlag, München 1994. *Grundlagen des klassischen Tanzes* (English title: *Basic Principles of Classical Ballet*) by Agrippina J. Vaganova – Henschel Verlag, Berlin 2002. *Schule des klassischen Tanzes* by Vera S. Kostrowitzkaja – Henschel Verlag, Berlin 2003.

Picture credits

The Painter

In the photo you can see me in conversation with the painter Christina Norström Blankstein. In her choice of pictorial themes, colours and dynamic, she is often inspired by dance and by dancers. As she is the mother of a dancer, she has a particularly intimate connection to the world of dance. I have been the subject and the inspiration of several of her paintings. Through some of these pictures, which she has very kindly put at my disposal or even specially created for the making of this book, I wanted to illustrate the way in which dance is perceived and interpreted in other art forms, how movement and mood can be conveyed, even by an immobile picture.

Christina Norström Blankstein was born and grew up in Sweden. Following her university studies in Geneva, she moved with her family to the United States. She currently lives and paints in Berlin. Christina Norström Blankstein started her career as a portraitist. Later, she combined realistic and abstract compo- nents in her work. She credits the harsh, magnificent landscapes of Arizona with its intense colour palette for much of her inspiration. Her current work is dedicated with powerful expressiveness to the dynamic tension of the human body in transition between stillness and movement.

The Author

Angela Reinhardt was born in Berlin and received her dance training at the National Ballet School, Berlin, studying with Nina Viktorovna Belikova and Prof. Martin Puttke, among others. In 1983 Tom Schilling engaged her directly as a dancer in the company of the Komischer Oper in Berlin. She was promoted to Soloist in 1985, and in 1987 she became the Principal Dancer of the company.

Whether in Berlin or on tour all over the world, Angela Reinhardt has always enjoyed exceptional success in the title rôles of Tom Schilling's perceptive and sensitive ballets, *Swan Lake, Romeo & Juliet, Cinderella* or *Elective Affinities.* She has also enchanted audiences and critics in the leading rôles of modern dance works by other choreographers. In this context one must mention the rôles of Marie in *Wozzeck, Maria Stuart, Salome* or *Coppélia.* Her ability to transform herself completely, her subtle balletic expressiveness and her masterly technique have all received high praise. Angela Reinhardt played the leading rôle in the television ballet film *Magdalena Eigner* and has appeared in many other films. Since 2002 she has been working as a freelance dancer and teacher.

During her dancing career, Angela Reinhardt has received numerous national and international prizes. Particularly noteworthy among these are the coveted First Prize of the *Johnson Foundation Prize* at the Prix de Lausanne in 1983, the Bronze Medal at the International Pas de Deux Competition in 1987 in Osaka, Japan, with Gregor Seyffert, and in the same year the "Bobby" television prize for Best Pas de Deux.

To date, in the course of her dancing career, Angela Reinhardt has worn and adapted some 2,000 pairs of pointe shoes. If you put all these shoes end to end in a single line, it would stretch to nearly 900 metres.